EDITOR

FIONA SAMPSON

Poetry adapts itself with enthusiasm to t[   ]   ⎽⎻ ⌄⎽⎻⌄extremity. "Our tempestuous day", "Things fall apart; the centre cannot hold", "History is now and England": Percy Bysshe Shelley, W.B. Yeats and T.S. Eliot are already there before us when we contemplate this summer's riots, and other disasters and disorders. Some of this may be a poetic assumption of the duties of unacknowledged legislation, as our uncannily premonitory last issue saw. Undeniably, some of it is simply a matter of rising to the excitement of the occasion.

But, in the face of mob rule, poetry's rugged individualism seems especially important. It offers its alternative, a kind of focused integrity. The understanding that we do not need to be totalizing, or totalitarian, but write all the more tellingly when we acknowledge our own particularity, is nowhere better illustrated than in Glyn Maxwell's subtle, reflexive 'Come to Where I'm From'. His extended meditation on being from Welwyn Garden City closes the 'Poems' section of this issue. Meanwhile, Hugo Williams's love poems are characteristically wry and intimate, John Burnside conjures his own unique tone-world in 'Alcools', and Fanny Howe's St Francis is a deeply vulnerable figure, sanctified in part by the scapegoating he undergoes. None of these figures is a sound-bite hero, or a rabble-rousing manipulator. Yet, how they resonate.

Elsewhere in this issue, *The Furthest Reach* becomes purely geographical; elsewhere still, it has to do with the kind of testing explorations that living with technology requires – as Gwyneth Lewis's discussion piece points out – and, in Maitreyabandhu's title essay, with poetry as a form of meditation. ...Up, down and sideways, poetry seems to be on satisfyingly polymorphous form, reaching the places that other forms of writing arguably can't. In my first *PR* editorial, I argued "against Balkanisation", the state of mutual entrenchment between different poetics which still dominated British poetry six or seven years ago. *PR*, with its usual vigorous mix of newcomers (one fifth of all poems and reviews we published last year were by emerging writers, who hadn't yet published a book) and distinguished poets from this country and abroad, has been working steadily since then to break down those barriers and resistances, and open up a field of poetry in which everyone is allowed to write in the way that suits them best. And British poetry is changing. ...How far, I wonder, can it reach?

A POEM FOR AI WEIWEI

Yang Lian
A Sunflower's Seed's Lines Of Negation

unimaginable that Du Fu's little boat was once
moored on this ceramic river
I don't know the moonlight   see only the poem's clarity
attenuated line by line   to a non-person
to the symbols   discussing and avoiding everything
I'm no symbol   a sun dying under the sunflower seed's hard shell
nor is the sun   snow-white collapsed meat of children
nor have I disappeared   daybreak's horizon impossibly
forgot that pain   bones like glass sliced by glass
I didn't scream, so must scream at each first light
an earthquake never stands still
no need to suffocate the dead   planting rows of fences to the ends of the earth
handcuffing ever more shameful silence   so   I don't fear
the young policewoman interrogating my naked body
it was formed by fire   no different to yours
knowing no other way to shatter but a hundred millions shatterings within myself
falling into no soil   only into the river that can't flow
that cares nothing for the yellow flower within the stone   having to go on
to hold back   like a drop of Du Fu's old tears
refusing to let the poem sink into dead indifferent beauty

Translated by Brian Holton and W. N. Herbert

Contents

Volume 101:3 Autumn 2011

Editorial

A Poem For Ai Weiwei

| 2 | Yang Lian | A Sunflower's Seeds's Lines Of Negation |

Poems

6	John Burnside	Alcools
10	Lizzi Thistlethwayte	I Will Break
11	Anne Stevenson	How Astonishing –
12	Hugo Williams	Tempera
		Love Poem
		Early Morning
		Hotel
		One Summer
17	Sean Borodale	Lyrigraph For The Upper Mells Stream (Damp Night)
18	John Mole	After Rain
19	Alan Brownjohn	Purchase
20	I. Galleymore	Turn Of Phrase
21	Ahren Warner	Hello London
		IX. Between
		XVIII. Before

The Furthest Reach

24	Seni Seneviratne	False Bay, Cape Town
25	Gerard Smyth	A Long Story
26	Maria Jastrzębska	The Major, Ealing 1959
28	Alyson Hallett	Finding Something Important In Istanbul
29	Eugene Dubnov	All My Russia
31	Kevin Crossley-Holland	Hammershøi
32	John Fuller	Cross-bones
34	Emily Berry	Bad New Government
35	Robert Saxton	The Roof Of The World
36	Malika Booker	Sue Speaks To Me In The Swan Room

37	Siriol Troup	Via Flaminia
	Anthony Dunn	Torch Song
38	Judith Kazantzis	What We Did In The Holidays
39	Olivia Byard	The Absent Thing (Good Friday at Pateley Bridge)
40	Kit Fan	Janus
41	Terry Jones	Trinities
42	Glyn Maxwell	Come To Where I'm From

Centrefold

51	Fanny Howe	In Prism
58	Maitreyabandhu	The Further Reach
70	Gwyneth Lewis	Poetry As Technology
75	ko ko thett & James Byrne	Bones Will Crow: A Selection Of Contemporary Burmese Poetry

Reviews

88	Steven Matthews on Geoffrey Hill and Derek Mahon
91	Chloe Stopa-Hunt reviews Sean O'Brien
93	Adam Thorpe on Jaan Kaplinski and Michael Longley
96	Kim Moore reviews Ruth Fainlight
98	Lavinia Singer on Bernard O'Donoghue and Mary Oliver
102	David Morley on Jovanović, Crowther and Kennelly
105	Tim Liardet on Warner, Ford, Lumsden and Pollard
108	Dai George on Berkeley, Crucefix, Nurske, Rudolf and Siddique
112	Tara Bergin on Lewis and Satyamurti
115	Molly Peacock reviews Liardet, Deane and Luther
118	Harriet Tarlo on Brading and Presley, Rich, Robertson and Williams
122	Sarah Wardle reviews debutants
124	Angel Dahouk on not giving up the day-job

POEMS

                                                        Even
Herr Haydn, Signor Boccherini, M. Saint-Saëns and Mr Elgar,
Long dead, are alive in those concertos I never quite learned to play
Before I listened to my deafness. This is my left foot, poetry.

                                                – Anne Stevenson

John Burnside
Alcools

I poison doux et chaste

The true griefs are eager as mink
and nothing consoles them,

no catalogue of mothering or sails,
no time and tide, no token of repentance.

Out in the yard,
at the near edge of mudslick and rain,

your skin wastes away
in its birdcage of milksop and rubble,

that stain where the mouth should be,
like unravelled yarn,

a cri-de-coeur, a toast,
a false confession,

your life as a hymn tune,
strung out on fish-hooks, like worms.

II noble et tragique

It's never the tragic and noble
you like to imagine,

this minor key of having been bereft
for years, before you chance upon a field
of mud and thistles in the summer rain

and see it clear: the weather of a heart
so commonplace, you think it must belong

to someone else.
There's nothing sweet and chaste: the actual poison
spreading in your blood is just a mix

of chalk and sugar, grains of powder-blue
and rose-red, while the life that was to come

is something on the wind, until the wind
decays along a wire of thorns and gravel.

III *Passons passons puisque tout passe*

I found a goldfinch
injured in the grass

and carried it into the house
for a moment's shelter.

It didn't live
and that was no surprise

but even as it faded
from the light

I felt its mercy,
something only half-

imagined, and more gift
than I can say,

grace being such a thing
as I find small

too readily, distracted from the light
of what there is

by what it was
I wanted.

IV *le bruit parmi le vent*

They say there are children, still,
in the furthest meadows.

In hollows of chalk and moon
they make their beds

from Lady's-smock
and strands of Old Man's Beard;

like pilgrims turned away
from blessèd knucklebones

or locks of hair,
they have that look

of having come too far
to be forgiven.

Beguiled by their vita nuova,
I love them well

and bait my snares for them
on warm nights, when the wind is like a veil

between the apple orchard
and the field;

and they have come
to love me well enough

to stay clear of my traps
till morning,

when I go out at first light
and gather in the shadows they have left

like hints of pike
and wolfskin in the grass,

wisps of the new life
snagged between trigger and spear.

THE TIMES
CHELTENHAMFESTIVALS

LITERATURE 11

in association with
waterstone's

7   16 OCTOBER 2011
BOX OFFICE 01242 505 444
REGENT ARCADE CHELTENHAM
cheltenhamfestivals.com
Go online for more info & to buy tickets

Costa Book of the Year 2010 winner Jo Shapcott guest directs
the 'Stanzas' programme, with a selection of events celebrating
the best of contemporary poetry.

HIGHLIGHTS

CAROL ANN DUFFY & JOHN SAMPSON
An unmissable evening of poetry and music with Poet Laureate
Carol Ann Duffy and musician John Sampson.

NATIONAL POETRY COMPETITION
Join the 2010 winners of this much-coveted prize as they read their winning entries.

BYRON
Distinguished poet Paul Muldoon offers a passionate
introduction to one of our most important poets.

WENDY COPE
This much-loved poet discusses her new collection
Family Values, the first for ten years.

DAVID HARSENT, SEAN O   BRIEN & PAUL MULDOON
Live poetry from three of Britain's finest poets.

PLUS visit the Poetry Café every weekday for more live readings.

10 DAYS
500 EVENTS
600 SPEAKERS
ONE AWFULLY
BIG ADVENTURE
visit cheltenhamfestivals.com

Lizzi Thistlethwayte
I Will Break

I will break lunch or is it
bread I will break bread and put cheese a dish of herbs
a glass of water
how lovely these reflective things how lovely
where the burst catkins
where the wings have slowed their creaking
where a flaw

and touching one another

Anne Stevenson
How Astonishing –

That this is my wild left foot I'm freeing from a Lycra sock,
That these arthritic fingers once belonged to my bow hand,
Slaves to a cello named Caesar and to Johann Sebastian Bach
Whose solo suite Number 5 in C minor, the Sarabande,
Is quietly fingering my memory: resignation and truth.
That I can lean over, flick a switch and a light will go on
Surprises me, as does nodding to sleep, book in hand, and flicking it off
To revive in the dark a young cello-playing Anne Stevenson
Along with strict Mr Troostewick (Troosey) in New Haven
And soft-spoken Mr Edel, feared and adored in Ann Arbor,
Both by now dead – living souls in beautiful instruments. Even
Herr Haydn, Signor Boccherini, M. Saint-Saëns and Mr Elgar,
Long dead, are alive in those concertos I never quite learned to play
Before I listened to my deafness. This is my left foot, poetry.

Hugo Williams
Tempera

It should have been all right
to think of her breaking eggs
for experiments with tempera,
getting her fingers dirty,
getting it in her hair.

It should have been okay
to remember her skipping
for no particular reason
when she walked beside me in the street.

Now that I've watered the rubbish
and put the flowers out,
there is nothing left to be done
but to stop in my tracks
and look in the palm of my hand.

Love Poem

I suppose you're right and breaking up
would be quite a good thing,
but staying together
would be an equally good thing,
so whatever we decide to do
it will be all right. On balance,
I lean towards doing nothing,
but whatever happens we'll go on
seeing each other, won't we?

I suppose it wouldn't be so bad,
seeing other people for a change,
we might even find someone
we could bear to be with
for more than half an hour,
although I doubt it somehow.
Experience suggests we go on
feeling the same about everything
no matter what happens. I do anyway.

Early Morning

Perhaps if I lie still
watching the tops of trees
scratching low clouds
I won't remember
her bedside manner,
her sense of etiquette.

If I let that branch
sweep the storm
into a corner of the sky
I might forget
the satisfaction she takes
in getting it just right.

If I watch that crow
flicking scrawls of black ink
from the edges of its wings
I might not remember
her saying certain things,
her throwing out one arm.

In a difficult dream
I was allowed to touch her hair.

Hotel

Our room was a summer birdcage
swinging from a hook
on the sunny side of the street.
Someone must have hung it there one day
and forgotten to bring it in.

We weren't complaining.
There was nothing under our feet
and nothing to hold on to,
but we liked the sensation
of swaying to and fro in the breeze.

One Summer

Two hot days and nights,
then a thunderstorm after you've gone.
I count the miles
between the lightning flash
and the first rumblings,
as the storm sets off northwards,
"looking for a place to lie down".

Car alarms moan in the distance.
A curtain of rain hangs in the garden,
then blows indoors.
I run upstairs to check the windows
and there it is –
the one in the bathroom still open
from when you were here.

Sean Borodale
Lyrigraph For The Upper Mells Stream (Damp Night)

The night is the wind wading itself.

I listen to the steep part of the valley
treading the dolomite.

The noise of trees shakes tambourines
as long as it takes to incorporate the trace

the noise of doors, shutting, opening

out flies an owl from a day of digestive sleep
patterns of wind, feathers

adjust responses to degrees
the give and take between two eyes

is that *your* torch, lightbeam, river
iron-rich rivulets are cables in the mud

water from the fields
touch and add –

the night, the wind wading itself, or what?
I listen, wide as a chantry door

for the noise to say ... and now the black
black stone of the hour

I think, I think, like time
turned heavy, thick

undress. walk over the boards of this house.
exit the river. whoever you are. lie down in this

John Mole
After Rain

Walking around the block
to shrug off weariness
and notice perhaps
how a letterbox shines
or gutters drip,

how the fishbone skeleton
of an aerial swims
in a black cloud
and a doorstep cat
has resumed its watch,

is to come back
into language, the promise
of finding words
for company
and what the sun can do.

Alan Brownjohn
Purchase

He believes he is awake, but no he isn't.
He is still in the dream, and admits that, saying aloud,
"I am dreaming this, and in a clammy sweat.
And what is the origin of 'clammy'?"

Then someone is closing the door, he knows
It's his real bedroom door from the sound of it.
His former partner is coming across the floor
Towards the bed. She gets into it beside him.

"Where did you go to be so late?" he asks,
With a yawn that almost forces him back to sleep.
Without a word she clambers over him into
Her usual sleeping position for several years.

He is conscious, very conscious, of dreaming now
Because a second shape has entered the room
By the same means, and entered the bed on the side
Still vacant, asking, "Who is that English woman?"

He is vulnerable enough to feel trapped by this.
"I have the assurance that I *can* wake up,
When the dream has reached closure," he thinks.
"But I haven't the least idea how to get it there.

"Through several layers of subconsciousness
I circle round in nightmare. The door has vanished
And yet, after months of sweating travel
I have reached it at last. I grip the handle,

"But my hand is clammy and slipping. Purchase on
The handle of anything has never proved
So hard... Except, I've done it. It turns. It opens.
I am there in the bed again. I hear the door."

I. Galleymore
Turn Of Phrase

After Francis Ponge's The Cycle of Seasons

A bud comes forth from the throat
and stuffs the mouth with an expression:
a dandelion head about to burst open,
a leaf furled like a new shaving brush.

The buds think they say everything afresh.

By the same unfolding and bright yellow gesture
they only say *leaf*, they only say *flower*.

Believing they've failed to make themselves heard
they grow taller and bigger and so lose their form.

They tire. The mouth that opened for them
dries up. That which was said, so eagerly,
now discolours, withers and drops.

Ahren Warner
Hello London

Just as – shifting the Double-Gauss a notch – the clarity attained is not
        what appears, but how what appears does,

so *l'étranger* is not this man in the window just off the Euston Road,
        but rather a shifting in this me that is.

And, what held for Louis holds true for me. In my teens, you were
        'foreign names over winking doors';

marred, perhaps, but only by the Thames' mean gust, slate-stolid *réveil*,
        that bite I came to need.

Still, it's been years since I came to you, a little less since you began
        to nibble, then gnaw, then masticate.

I don't know if I got out or was spat. But, somehow, I'm back: transient,
        for now, a fleeting whiff,

amuse-gueule, faint stirring of your parotid. Soon, I promise to be
        here – at your leisure, to lick and lap –

        your spittle shiver now blain, now numb dread.

IX. Between

the *barre* and the *grand battement en cloche*,
      the *en dedans*
and the *en dehors* of last night's night-off
      fuckathon –

her room at the Grand Hotel, the *première*
      danseuse
and me (mere *sujet*) grinding through first
      to fifth

and on to two positions in which she led,
      never
myself having studied – under or on top of –
      J.G. Noverre.

XVIII. Before

Soutine had left Smilovitch, had left Minsk, had left Vilnius.
   Long
before Soutine had left Paris, left Céret, had left Paris
   again,

before he had left Champigny, slept rough in the forest:
   a Jew,
and Slav; trying to avoid his *billet simple* to Auschwitz.
   And,

therefore, even longer before his hematemesis,
   the blood
chucked up, the ulcer that ruptured, the peritonitis,
   the covert

agony of a night-time drive, northwards, towards Paris;
   the success
of avoiding the Gestapo. Thus, long before Soutine's
   exsanguination:

the *bobo* idyll of *Le Bateau-Lavoir*, its half-starved artists.
   Et après?
Matisse, radiance of crepe, cancer smarting like a bitch.

Seni Seneviratne
False Bay, Cape Town

And how do I rinse out the Indian ocean blue of her?
Is it as obvious as following the cycles of the moon

or burning sandalwood and chamomile to wake up
one day and not think of her, to redraw the line of trees

on Signal Hill? I sleep with an arched back and bent knees,
my feet in starting blocks all night. And what I have to say

is spilled paint on the highway, the footprints of a bird
without wings, the crickle of bamboo against a window pane,

a kiss in a doorway in an etching of Venice. I'm heading for
the Bridge of Sighs and the space anyone might fall back into.

The present persists, so light of things and yet so heavy.
I wear my disappointments like a coat. It has many pockets.

Gerard Smyth
A Long Story

It's a long story between Gregorian chant
and the beats of electronica:
there's the featherweight sonata
on which we drift away,
the fecundity of Mozart,
adagios of Mahler, the back-to-back
lives of Schubert and Brahms
with their symphonies of strings and brass.

It's a long story
between Vienna's fairytale waltz
and *The Fairytale of New York*,
between Bach and modern jazz:
Bach, the keeper of flocks,
of places where sheep could safely graze.
The *Art of Fugue*, its coming of age,
passed on but the Art of Fugue became
music for the hour of rapture,
the sound of wheels on fire.

THE 23RD INTERNATIONAL ALDEBURGH POETRY FESTIVAL
4–6 November 2011
Programme with this edition of Poetry Review
Join our mailing list
info@thepoetrytrust.org

THE POETRY TRUST

THE COMPLETE POETRY WEEKEND
25 poets from all over the UK and beyond, including
Fleur Adcock, Robert Hass (USA)
Roger McGough & Kay Ryan (USA)

52 EVENTS, 14 FREE
BOOKING OPENS 5 SEPTEMBER

www.thepoetrytrust.org

Maria Jastrzębska
The Major, Ealing 1959

Slicked parting, short back and sides, always in shirts and slacks
the Major, a family friend, has a bed-sit on the ground floor.

(Three or four Warsaw apartments could fit in your grandmother's
house. It smells of floor wax, Harpic toilet cleaner. Sometimes

you're allowed to go upstairs where the other lodgers live,
see the light shining through green stained glass in the lavatory.)

The garden stretches out. You lose count of the trees,
Comice, plum, Worcester, Discovery, walnut, mulberry.

The Major's glueing soldiers together, twelve packs for a shilling.
Sometimes black and white cows, green windmills, tractors, barns.

Indoors you play with the soldiers – your favourites in grey uniforms,
round helmets. You line them up next to the Indians with their bows

and arrows and the silver knights on horseback. But your army
is outnumbered. Encircled by tank divisions that advance

across the linoleum. Fired on by flying artillery. You're running
across fields on the old Persian rug to capture canons, fortresses.

Charge! You don't stand a chance. You're wounded
crawling under the table. Drag yourself to the Major's door, ajar today.

Peeping in, pull yourself up, stand to attention. Voices talking.
Cups rattle on saucers. The Major has visitors. Three ladies.

You're waiting to give your report. They carry on talking, dipping spoons
of jam into their tea. *Not today, soldier*, says the Major

looking up at last. *About turn!* As you walk slowly away you hear
the major's voice: *Soldiers never cry. Ba-aczność! Lewa, prawa.*

∗

When the Major dies they lay her out in uniform
with all the medals, but you're not allowed to see her.

At night she appears in your room. You sit up in bed. You knew it!
Knew all along! She isn't dead, but the operation

must be kept strictly secret. Soldiers honour. *Promise?*
Of course. She salutes you with a shiny robotic arm

and on her new mechanical legs – *Ba-aczność! Lewa, prawa.*
Spocznij! – marches away swiftly through the dark.

Ba-aczność – atten-tion
Lewa – left
Prawa – right
Spocznij – at ease

Alyson Hallett
Finding Something Important In Istanbul

It wasn't the magnificent Galata Bridge
and the hundreds of men fishing
in the middle of the day in the middle of the city.
It wasn't the Topaki Palace or the great round trays
of honeyed and pistachioed baklava. It wasn't
the roof-top table where we ate breakfast
or the flotilla of ships on a sun-kissed Bosphorous,
not even the Blue Mosque or the Hagia Sophia
or the café in the graveyard and that sweet
apple tea. It was the nameless place
where we waited for a ferry to Fener.
An old man offering us two rickety seats
under a blue plastic sheet and an older man
making us two cups of instant coffee.
The skinny cat and bob of boats,
grubby table and diesel fumes.
Not the sights you must see
but the oversights, the ones you're told to avoid.
Something beautiful exploding between
one thing and another, the plastic sheet
and the sky, the rubbish in the water
and the smile on the old man's face.

Eugene Dubnov, translated by Anne Stevenson
All My Russia

In the film I was watching there were flying cranes;
Men for the front were leaving their girls grief-numbed
On that part of earth – most memorable – that remains
The motherland where I was born and named.

My eyes kept shifting from the TV screen
To the photo-portraits hanging over it,
That row of leaders' faces with obscene
Scowling jowls, all seeming to connect

In one clenched tragedy of terror and misery,
Cynicism and submission. And suddenly
It became for the first time clear to me
This picture was all my Russia, locked in me.

Literal translation: Iambic pentameter rhyming abab

I was watching a film: cranes were flying,
Volunteers were abandoning their girls
In that part – most memorable – of the earth
Where I was born and named.

From the TV screen my glance
Kept all the time shifting to the portraits
Of the leaders hanging over it – to the row
Of the rulers' heavy faces – and that

Interplay of tragedy and evil,
Of cynicism and submission* was revealed
To me so clearly for the first time – and this picture**
Was all of my Russia.

* Submissiveness, resignation.
** As in English, both a movie and a view/scene/spectacle.

Original

Евг. Дубнов

ВСЯ МОЯ РОССИЯ

Я видел фильм: летели журавли,
Любимых добровольцы покидали
В той части - самой памятной - земли,
Где я родился и мне имя дали.

С экрана телевизора мой взгляд
Переходил все время на портреты
Вождей, над ним висевшие, на ряд
Тяжелых лиц правителей - и эта

Взаимосвязь трагедии и зла,
Цинизма и покорности впервые
Открылась мне так явственно: была
Картина эта - вся моя Россия.

N.B. This poem was written when the author worked for the BBC Monitoring Service and watched Soviet Television.

Kevin Crossley-Holland
Hammershøi

Where there is brightness, it's always beyond,
on the other side of the wide window
– and so, by inference, before or after,
anyhow elsewhere. She waved her wand
and banished it all a long time ago.

A long time, is it? She scarcely knows.
To and fro she rocks, to and fro,
waiting while silence advances on us
and we see what she sees indoors
and out, stealthy as falling snow.

Where's that pin? She was holding it between
her bony fingers just a moment ago.

John Fuller
Cross-bones

Grown older, and feeling the first signs of muscular fatigue, I have come to think more and more about the long traditions of the box. It isn't that I fear failure, or want to change anything. Really, I am quite happy with the box, and no amount of temporary stiffness (alarming as it sometimes is) would persuade me into making it slightly larger. But as these thoughts occur to me, only to be comfortably put to one side, I am left remembering that great decision of my youth, not at the outset to relax the given conditions in the timidity of my inexperience (which would have been perfectly understood, and immediately forgiven) but in fact to make the box smaller.

There is no concealing the fact that despite the personal satisfaction of entering the box, such that a performance needs no witness, no wonder, and no applause, it is in reality an intensely competitive business. To inherit the tradition is to accept a challenge that will be fiercely scrutinised by one's peers. One tiny miscalculation and one would never hear the end of it. A failure in performance would have been unthinkable. You will see, then, that at the outset a small adjustment in one's favour would be an understandable preparation for a lifetime of selfless devotion, by no means a subterfuge, hardly a weakness.

But to make the act harder, and from the very beginning! Did this imply an overweening confidence in the years of private preparation? Perhaps it might be taken as a criticism of the tradition I had inherited. It might be acknowledged with a grudging admiration as belonging to the natural effrontery of the young. My predecessors had learned to make a great rigmarole of increased bondage, as though only the tightest of straps could assist something as unwieldy as a naturally muscular human body into the confines of a crimson metal box less than two feet cubed. But I carelessly abandoned the harness altogether, while reducing the size of the box by visible inches.

The daring of it made my heart beat faster. At the first performance I left one arm quite outside the box. It waved cheerfully at the onlookers and pushed my head this way and that way as though it had no idea what to do with it, while the head glared back at the bullying arm in comic resentment. I made it seem that there was no room for my skull in the box, which was demonstrably chock-full of my already carefully folded cross-bones. And even if there had been, how could the arm have possibly followed it?

Well, there was an answer, and it lay in the dislocation of more bones than my nearest rivals had ever thought it possible to dislocate. And this, too, without the secret assistance of the harness. All was done naturally with small, barely noticeable twitches and jerks of the body under the cover of exaggerated stretches and yawns, as though I were simply preparing for a comfortable night's rest. The folding and inserting of the limbs certainly looked perfectly natural, and was accomplished with a fluid movement while talking happy rubbish to the onlookers. I made it seem like the easiest thing in the world.

But what is it about an audience that makes them so fickle? What is it that upsets them? They laughed at my disrobing. They laughed at my skeletal body. They laughed at the to-and-fro between my evasive and reluctant head and the commandeering arm.

Once entirely in the box, however, once my disappearing fingers had finally flipped down the lid, I failed to please them. They looked again at the tiny box left isolated on the stage, and could hardly believe that I was inside. Yes, they had seen me fold myself inside, but now that I was no longer visible it did not seem possible. There must be some trick. But they could not see what the trick was.

It was not even like a suitcase. Women have been dismembered, and their remains left at the Lost Property Offices of railway stations in suitcases. But this was so small! It was little more than a hat box, or the container of a chamber-pot. And when my assistant came to take it away, hoisting it under his arm with an ostentatious little grunt, and pretending to stagger, their confusion was complete.

'We saw him get in,' they said. 'The floor there is solid. There is no trapdoor. And yet... and yet he surely cannot be in that tiny box!'

I could hear the general murmur and wonderment, and it had a strange effect on me, as though I had indeed achieved an impossible disappearance. As though one minute I had been myself, erect, articulate, conversational, and then suddenly had been folded away into nothing. As though I were not in the box after all. And because I had no means of revealing myself, and was from then on entirely at the mercy of my assistant, it hardly seemed to matter where I was. He could have walked away with me into another life, or abandoned me, like one of those Lost Property victims.

This successful removal from life is a rare thing. It has been achieved by a few saints and holy men, and perhaps by some others for whom the body has become, when all is said and done, something of an embarrassment.

Emily Berry
Bad New Government

Love,   I woke in an empty flat   to a bad new government;
it was cold   the fridge was still empty   my heart, that junkie,
was still chomping on the old fuel   *vroom*, I start the day like a tired
        motorcyclist   I want to go very fast and email you about the following
happy circumstances: early rosebuds, a birthday party, a new cake recipe   but
    today it's hot water bottles and austerity breakfast and my toast burns in protest

        You are not here of course but you live in me like a tiny valve of a man
you light up my chambers   Later I will call to tell you about the new
        prime minister,   the worrying new developments   and about how
I am writing my first political poem   which is also (always) about my love for you

Robert Saxton
The Roof Of The World

Imagine being a nun on a plateau
among lamas – if there's a lovelier life
I'd like to know. High above hills of tea
her cup's the sky, her brew's a solitary leaf

some porter brought and slipped into her prayers,
her dreams being locked. One door of the chapel
releases a prism of bright surprise.
A Himalayan morning greets her pearl –

red bull let loose among milk-swollen cows
that rub the sleep of ages from their eyes,
with hooves – a miracle that lifts the curse
from beasts not born to touch themselves with ease.

FARRINGFORD
HOLIDAY COTTAGES
In a setting so inspiring, Tennyson lived there for **40** years

The breathtaking walks, fresh sea air and peace and quiet make the Farringford Estate on the historic Isle of Wight the ideal academic's retreat. Former home to Poet Laureate, Alfred, Lord Tennyson, Farringford is set in the tranquil seclusion of 100 acres of beautiful countryside. Nestled within the grounds are the immaculate 2-bedroom Alfred & Emily cottages, fully equipped for self-catering; the Alfred's boast vaulted ceilings, stone fireplaces and wood-burning stoves. There is also a restaurant championing sustainable local produce with an award-winning chef at the helm. The magnificent colours of the flora & fauna and endless empty beaches during Autumn/Winter make it the perfect time to stay. Open all year for holidays and short breaks; family friendly, pets welcome.
Special offers for long lets.

+44(0)1983 752 500 • WWW.FARRINGFORD.CO.UK
FARRINGFORD, BEDBURY LANE, FRESHWATER BAY, I.O.W. PO40 9PE

Malika Booker
Sue Speaks To Me In The Swan Room

Now we're old parrots, who have lost their flair,
we've no stories to tell. Back then we were red
breasted robins; bright Dolly, chirpy Chrissie,
flighty Stella and me. No boys on our horizons then.
We were children thinking ourselves grown up, in love
with Shakespeare, this stage, the actors, the dust.
Back then we were blue tits, bright turtle-necks,
A-line mini skirts and knee length boots.
Back then we stood by roadsides, fists mid-air,
thumbs cocked up hitching rides. Back then
we hoarded pocket money for tickets, too poor
to take the bus. We'd ride from Coventry
in Ford Austins, Mini Minors or Cortinas.
Back then it was safe. At the Theatre we queued
for hours, flasks of tea warming our palms,
bare knees cold, for one & sixpence tickets,
then stood at the back for a three hour play.
If our money stretched to two seats we sat
on each other's knees the entire time.
After we'd camp in a tent by the river,
cold little nesting birds, squeezed. Back then
I loved Olivier. His voice, slicked back hair.
Oh he was tall, could charm the pants off me
any day. No man ever measured up to that one,
not even my husband. All these years
we've migrated to return each new season,
until Dolly flew away. It was sudden flight.
That cup of tea and empty chair is Dolly's.

Siriol Troup
Via Flaminia

Lightning flickers on the hills, wasps
crater the plums. Madness to leave
the superstrada striking through the cliffs
and take this cranky Roman pass
cut deep in the gorge – the little forum
where we find ourselves ducking
the sun's aim, strung along sheer rock
by engineers of hope while time traps
Vespas and Vespasian in its flow.
Beyond the river's chloroform bend
the land smells of polecats,
woolly oaks, yellow-bellied toads.
Shivered with spray, the future roars.

Antony Dunn
Torch Song

                          She is
so pleased to discover that
those astronauts had planted
cats' eyes across the near side
of the moon –
                 if you catch her
on her back on the night-lawn
with a strong torch she will be
testing quite how far from things
she is

Judith Kazantzis
What We Did In The Holidays

Some of us, rightly or wrongly, thought that the town
        had seen things it shouldn't,
we may have exaggerated the smell, the sweetish smell
        that crept up through the floor
of the kitchens. We suddenly wondered if we were baking
        our own thighs, oblivious, I mean,
still on in our stoves. At that point, nauseated, we felt we
        should drive to the seaside
to catch pure air, our ozone gift, our toffee brown seaweed,
        our miniature life forms,
delicacies delectable and quaint in the fingernail tide pools.

C.K. Williams' 'Whacked' in a stunning limited edition

To mark the occasion of the 2011 Poetry Society Annual Lecture, the Poetry Society has produced a limited edition print of C.K. Williams' tour de force poem 'Whacked'

Featuring striking woodcuts by the artist and former *Daily Telegraph* political cartoonist Nicholas Garland, the edition was printed by Phil Abel of Hand & Eye letterpress studio, London. Set in Plantin on a 200gsm Fabriano paper, the print (folded to 297 x 200 mm) is published in an edition of just 450, making it the perfect souvenir and gift this Christmas.

Non-members: £12
Poetry Society members: £8
Signed copies are available at no extra charge while stocks last.

BUY ONLINE at **http://www.poetrysociety.org.uk/shop/product/401/**

Olivia Byard

The Absent Thing
(Good Friday at Pateley Bridge)

Near noon,
a long straggle of believers
with brass players and a muffled drum
follow a priest carrying
a bare wooden cross.
But the road's
not closed, so they're snarled at
by pent-up four-by-fours.

This remnant
procession crosses the road
for the final minutes
of prayers and hymns, harried
from behind by revving cars,

and we escape uphill:
to an old kiln and a curlew's call
splintered by rumble; as
up from the fierce melée below –
a discharge

Kit Fan
Janus

of the front door yet to be repainted
probably this spring in deep green; of
the porch door newly painted in a draft-
washed white; of the kitchen door ajar
smell of a pork shoulder roasting in garlic
and fennel seeds; of the cat flap reserved
for the sleek, handsome Pantalaimon
and regally neurotic Aphrodite; of
concrete and abstract things like change
passages
          transitions
               like climbing up
the stairs to discover the things within
human control like frame within frame
the variations of blue and sea that make
the beak of a hummingbird true for a curlew
and the things beyond like an unexpected
phone call on a Sunday morning disrupted
lovemaking, the loss and tears that follow,
thoughts of exit and entrance clouding over
the mind on a cold sunny day where everything
has a shadow to make meaning of.

Terry Jones
Trinities

That we have to breathe   exhale in the world   to live in the world

That we eat the world   its plants and flesh   digest the world

That we build here   name localities   congregate the world

That we have imagined it   speak it   in all languages

That we have designs   world blueprints   books of the world

That we library world   shelf it   consult it

That now and here   set as it is   we must turn it

palgrave
macmillan

"I'm not sure that any book has ever truly changed my life in the sense of dramatically altering its course, but I can think of one that determined it, and that's Palgrave's Golden Treasury."
- Howard Jacobson

www.palgrave.com

Forewood by Carol Ann Duffy

The Golden Treasury

Paperback | October 2011 | £12.99

Glyn Maxwell
Come To Where I'm From

Hard to remember, now there is nothing here,
that there was once nothing here. Hard to remember
they paused in a field with a plot for a field and a feel
of a place in mind and a little knot of horses
      faraway in a corner stood there

pretty much where that little knot of horses
stands. The railway ran through the white template,
the life and death of it, made east and west
of nowhere. North and south it left itself
      whichever way one looked.

Hard to remember now that it's all begun
that it all began and, now that it's all over,
hard to recall it's gone. Those who are gone
arrive in a crest of steam and the late-lamented
      help them with their boxes.

Those to the east have a shed and those to the west
a greenhouse, it was a field and not a field
hereafter, it was a path through new houses
and a sweetshop. There was a lane and another lane
      which, crossing it, was obliged

to name it what it was named and the five things
needed they built buildings for. A meadow
reared its set of gardens like farm-children
edging behind houses to belong there,
      to cluster and imagine

a gate that is always shut will be always open.
But for now the horizon was sky and a blackberry hedge
and the north was the nettle-bed, and the south the roses
and the east an archway to those sad allotments,
      and the west a banded twilight

as out they build, in the time a bedtime story
takes to ferry me shipshape to tomorrow;
out they build till I wake and the horizon's
gone. It won't be found until it's wept to
      on a holiday. The town

is mine, this side of town is mine, the homes
go strolling by, then, bowing out of sight
they scurry round the world to be back in time
for when I pass, as if they never budged,
      and a chuckle of wood-chimes

is all I'll ever know. Now they grow names
with care, they name what dreams of being garden
Garden, what will never be a city
City, and they name it for some hovels
      in the Domesday Book. Go where

they say it is. Come to where I'm from.
The north is lost in thought: the glance away
from fairytales is a look through time, the south
is sitting me down and standing me up, the east
      unnerves me with its look:

I never heard of west, what's west? and the west
goes west in search of answers. Hard to remember
I know what I mean, now nothing's left but a lawn
and me knowing what I mean. The place spread out
      like anything being thought of

reddens in shame and joy. So I was thought of,
for the north was a copse of houses to be called at,
found wanting at, found wanting *you*, while the south
got London like one gets a belief and beamed
      to find it all leads somewhere.

The east I met in dreams was the east I knew
but enormous, so the west escorted me
where those like me *liked* me, on a singing bus-ride
I prayed would never end till I begged it to.
        Things come true, looking back,

things come true I was wishing for, they are gone
and still come true, when north south east and west
flop on a lawn in summer and so do you,
and the time I stare at you and you do
        are the same time, are equal,

the same time, same span, like an equals sign
is suddenly loop-the-looping home so it forms
infinity by a hedge in summer – *You,*
I caught your eye in my life. What else did I do?
        and the longer ago it gets

the longer it lasts and closer it seems to come.
Come to where I'll never again be from,
you, there are miracles showing up again
instead of us. The shadows comb the lawn,
        diligent and discreet

as a search team until I call it off
for want of a clue. South go the memories,
north goes love as I wake, while the east and west
welcome the bright apprentice and dispatch him
        daily on his amiable

fruitless errand. My eyes grow books and suffer
books, my ears grow songs and suffer songs,
my hands break news, my feet fetch drinks, my stomach
stomachs it all like something bet it it couldn't,
        and out they build, they build,

from the soft incessant fountain they began with,
to the homes we knew and will never, side by side
they build them, like the ones we won't remember
play tag in the park with the ones we can't forget
      and the kids they brought together

had kids together and soon the north was the poems
I wrote about you, woods of poems I pass through
guided by a voice in headphones, soon
the south is the realm of Alfie Rose, the east
      an airport serving nowhere

and the west the news I brush off like a boy-king
as I stir the foam and find I'm in Manhattan.
And maybe they built out far enough, I wonder,
sipping the wine in a brasserie I always
      loved, or I text my exes

in the terminal or I listen to the songs
I listen to. At the rendezvous of evening
I always miss for mulling over headlines,
what travelled outward travels at standstill,
      then starts to travel in,

when the woodland path arrives in the blue clearing:
the youngest lad of three is getting ready
to set some last adventure with his soldiers.
But his pals who don't take no for an answer shriek
      from the road until he rises,

childhood done forever. The clearing reached,
the path is weeds and litter. Hard to remember,
now I've everything, that I once had everything,
and I drive through a north I cried in, where the council's
      nailed up signs and arrows

that *These are trees* and *So are these*, and the south
is so far south it's south of understanding,
and the east is the internet and the west my time here
googled with a whisky. Come to where
       I said it was, it's there

I'm gone. The plastic infantryman
dropped in the wood outlasts the wood. I meet you
for the last time but one on a rainy Thursday,
and the street rolls up behind me like a script
       unless I turn to stop it.

The fine idea remains just that. The blueprint
flutters down unused, and the children's children
tweet on the ragged swings. There's not a tree,
a yard of light, a lamp-post that won't
       tap from me my only

soliloquy *I remember when we,*
when she, declining, like an old-school verb,
to *when you*. Then you, derailed at a dream-junction,
are someone else again, the old first names
       step out in their parish beauty,

Rosemary, Clare, Diane... What I want from one
is what I got from one, as if the maths
made sense in the negative: now writing looks
like black on white but feels like flint on nothing.
       North they are shutting up

the picture book forever, south the theatre's
pricey card for children, east the warehouse
eats the one beside it, west I set out
seats for relatives and replay scenes
       that happened in the west,

right there I mutter, peering into sunset,
pulling a cork among abandoned deck-chairs.
Come to where I'm from, like the bloke I once
got talking to in The Sun, on the only night
       he spent in my birthplace,

a desolate Sunday evening wiping tables
and he said *I hate it here* and he was gone,
said he'd never come again, come again like him,
when you never will, come to where I'm from
       like the glossy editor

in Soho who confided in me *Glyn,*
it does you no favours, saying where you're from:
say you're 'from Hertfordshire', come again like him,
where you wouldn't be seen dead. Come again like one
       who's lost, come again like one

for seconds on First Capital Connect,
who meant to lift his eyelids from his iPhone
as the little place shot by but when he looks
we're on Brunel's old viaduct, gone, bygone,
       high over the green fields

and lanes of where I'm from. The north is a new
flowerbed from who knows when, the south
four 4x4s on a driveway, in the east
a fellow stops to stare at where we lived
       as if he remembered us

when he lived, I remember him well enough, and the west
is me at work on this by the garden gate.
Preposterous, what was. I watch that gate
for you and all the gone. The odds against
       are stars to sail between.

Come to where I'm from. Now there's nothing here,
hard to remember once there was nothing here.
Hard to remember we paused in a field in sunshine
with a plot for a field and a feel of a place in mind
        and a little knot of horses

faraway in a corner stood right there
near where those horses stand, by the quiet trees,
beyond which all the yellow rising hills
you think are there are the yellow rising hills
        you thought were there.

 THE POETRY SOCIETY ANNUAL LECTURE **2011**

C.K. WILLIAMS
ON BEING OLD

Influential American poet C.K Williams, winner
of the Pulitzer Prize, travels to the University
of Liverpool to deliver the Poetry Society's
Annual Lecture 'On Being Old', given as this
year's Kenneth Allott Lecture. Interspersed
with dramatic new poems the lecture explores
his changing relationship with the great poets
of history, from Wyatt, Wordsworth and
Pushkin to Bishop, Auden and Lowell.

FREE EVENT
Thurs 13 October, 5pm

2011 Kenneth Allott Lecture
Leggate Theatre
Victoria Gallery and Museum
University of Liverpool

 UNIVERSITY OF
LIVERPOOL

To book, email: jgaywood@liverpool.ac.uk

Photo: Tineke de Lange

CENTREFOLD

Now we're upstream from ethics because we're in the
creative flow itself, where the rules inside the poem and
those outside aren't different as they are down here.

– *Gwyneth Lewis*

ADMISSION FREE

National Poetry Day Live
games

Thursday 6 October 2011
1pm-6pm

The **Poetry Society** and
Southbank Centre, London

Poetry Takeaway!

Poetry Bingo!

invite you... to roll up, pens at the ready, for one potato, two potato and conkers at 20 paces, at Southbank Centre, London, for National Poetry Day Live 2011. This year's theme is 'Games', with the Clore Ballroom as poetry's playground.

FREE LIVE performances from a host of poetry's famous names and rising stars including:

Poetry Doctor!

+ Simon Armitage
+ Jo Bell
+ Imtiaz Dharker
+ Laura Dockrill
+ Jackie Kay

SLAMbassadors
+ Joelle Taylor
+ Naga MC
+ Catherine Labiran

+ Glyn Maxwell
+ Michael Rosen
+ Jo Shapcott
+ Ahren Warner
+ Philip Wells

Foyle Young Poets
+ Helen Mort
+ Richard O'Brien

Poembola!

THE POETRY SOCIETY

VENUE
Royal Festival Hall foyers & Clore Ballroom
Southbank Centre, London SE1

For timings and further details, see www.poetrysociety.org.uk

In Prism

FANNY HOWE

for XB

In Umbria, pastel air clings to the mountains in veils of pink and mauve. Everything near the surface seems unusually soft, even the stones. Francis was born and died in Assisi, central Italy, around the turn of the twelfth century.

I have read that he was humiliated by his merchant father and ran off to join the military but got whooping cough and had to turn back. On the way he tried to save face by joining a subversive operation and ended up in prison for a whole year.
There, he stopped singing, speaking, or smiling.

For millennia people have wanted a God and a sky where knowledge and history are stored, so that when someone punched you or kicked you down the stairs and there was no one else but the evil one beside you, you could look up from the ground and say, "God knows what you have done."

It seems important that every act is known, even if it goes unpunished, I don't know why, or why the sky is the repository vault. The Pseudo Dionysus said that "the more distant the soul is from the body, the more available it is to the influx of spiritual substances."

The final encounter with his father describes Francis taking off all his clothes and standing naked in front of the angry man. Then he lay on the ground on his back as if he were laying his life down, the way lovers do, or having his body prepared for funeral rites. He pushed his heap of clothes towards his father, and then continued looking up.

I can hear nothing but birds from outside the open window and the bray of a donkey like the sound at the opening of Bresson's *Balthazar*.

In the seventies Cardinal Ratzinger silenced the Franciscan liberationist theologians. He called them secular heretics and ideologues who would damage the Church by teaching people to solve their own social problems. But the populace got angry, and he had to relent, and allow them to speak again of a religious humanism.

Just around the time of St. Francis, the Pope (Innocent) was obsessed with heretics and had the Cathars massacred in the Albigensian Crusade in France. This was a massacre like that at Masada, which was horrifying to even the most avowedly Catholic in the population. Women, children... but most memorably, the Cathars did not resist but stood their ground and held to their progressive beliefs.

Martyrs are not saints but they are certain. The Cathars held tight to many beliefs that Francis himself did, Francis who was called the Little Frenchman because of his love of French poetry, the moon, sun and bits of nature whom he addressed in the second person. Like him, the Cathars did not believe that love and power could coexist.

*

The first question in the Catechism is:
What was humanity born for?
To be happy is the correct answer.

Once Francis was on the road with his friends, he was happy. Up till then, the people in town threw rocks at him. They abused him as the children abused the priest in *Christ Stopped at Eboli*. They believed he was damaged already. They slapped mud on his face and hunched over, cackling at his surprise. They kicked him from behind, pushed him, and drew blood. This was when he began walking alone in his strange outfit, staring out in wonder.

One day he cast off the threads he was wearing and stood naked on the edge of the forest. The crowd saw the lacerations they had left on his body, and withdrew, embarrassed. This is the Glory part of the Mass I never composed, because when Francis looks at them with his lifted face, his cheeks are coloured by an explosion of clouds. Years later he would have his eyes cauterized by fire.

*

The curate, passing, asks children in a patronizing and suspicious voice:

What is God?

What do the Scriptures teach?

How did God create the world?

The curate moves forward with his lips pursed. In some way he resembles
Joseph in Pasolini's film about Jesus.
Joseph is suspicious of Mary. His lips tighten when he looks at her, but then
the angel comes and his lips soften.

Pavel Florensky in prison realized that gold was not a colour. John in prison
had his visions that emerged like the faces you see behind your sealed eyelids.

Francis wondered before the Pontiff:
Why do we want to learn how to live wisely?
We are just going to die.

For what purpose should we resist hitting people with our fists and spit?
And, without waiting for an answer, he did four somersaults.

*

A penny per footfall, is the rule of the world.

We all sat in the car leaving Assisi wondering about living in America. We had
all put in time over the years, trying to move the country into a more
humane and just democracy. Now not one of us could see much
improvement in education or health care, in housing or care for the planet.
The same division existed between those who feared the government and
those who trusted government as when we were young.

Rush hour between Assisi and Umbertide was mild and fast-moving on the
two lane highway. Hills and vineyards looping up and over themselves. How
orderly the old cypresses are, and how well this country seemed to
understand the relationship between the earth and the sky, was the other
topic of conversation.

In the tomb of St. Francis I saw a woman writhing and sobbing "Mamma Mia" on a bench, while the tourists filed past and the monks ignored her. She was pregnant. Was she in labour? Or over-stimulated by the presence of Francis entombed?

It was an atmosphere of cold dense ions and ash. In the little door to the upper chapel a monk sat on the floor singing the rosary. This chapel was set inside a giant imperial church, a little golden seed at the heart of stone.

I remembered Anna Magnani in *Mama Roma*, being so rough, so loud, so pushy, a force of nature. Like a stallion, her movements graceful and wild, her face receives every emotion without any intervention of a second thought.

The bored boys, brutal men, the motorbikes and helmets circle the statue of the Madonna, for they will die speeding.

"I love my mother," said the boy in the movie climbing up the post-War rubble with the girl.
"How do you know?" she asked.
"Because I would cry if she died."

Mamma Roma loved him and did everything to make him happy and to protect him, and look what happened.

Francis was rarely well. He carried several physical problems with him, his eyesight was increasingly weak. But he went ahead and lived with lepers for a time, and made sure his friars had enough to eat, usually a pot of unsalted vegetable soup that acquired a wonderful consistency when cooked with lumps of bread in it.

They slept under the stars or inside a cowshed near their church.

*

I will always associate Rome with a walnut.

That night I drank walnut liqueur, just a sip, it tasted like kahlua. The inner wing of a bird is the colour of a doe.
And the turned-over earth is the colour of a nut, and a bird, but soon it will

be watered for the green wheat of spring.

Flying up the hill on the back of the motorbike in the warm Roman air was like drinking from the fountain of youth.
Umbrella trees along the Tiber.

I walked on the rooftops across Rome, including a grassy one, and one where a palm grew out of a crack in the rocks.

I was carrying an assortment of envelopes containing paintings and notes for my Mass but they could not be managed easily because their shapes were irregular.
Some had juttings, some were swollen, the colour red was prominent. They depicted divided cities, divided into layers, not all in a line. A layer cake sagging under the weight of accumulated dust, dirt and now grass.

Each layer had been purchased at the cost of decades, even centuries of hand-hurting, back-breaking slave labor. *Caveat emptor!*
Broken columns, mashed marble friezes and faces. The triumph of greed was written across my storyboard. The city was a mighty and devouring creation, a creature with a crusted skin.

The air, the sun, the moon and a spark were the only places of serenity and enlightenment.

Even in the city you look for a place that welcomes you. You actually want to be found!
Being found is the polar opposite of making a vow.
No people are involved.

When you sit down on a stone, face up to the sun, you can't help but think *Mine, mine*. And you don't have to promise anything to anyone in time.
You may be called to a place of banality or genius, but as long as it is your own happiness that responds to it, you are available to something divine.
Mozart sat at the piano for the better part of every day.

All over the world monks have lived in desert hovels as scribes, prophets, mendicants. They are the extreme realization of one aspect of human personality that tends towards lack of possession and solitude.

People recognize them as authentic players, whether they are Zen or Christian.

On the other hand, "I don't believe a word of it," is what most people think when somebody who has power starts talking.

There was a hole in the roof of the Pantheon where we were told that the snow fell through onto the relics of Catherine of Siena the mystic and onto the porphyry.

St. Francis wept and stripped, laughed and lectured and called creation "you" all the way to the end. When he was dying he asked to be stripped naked to lie on the floor in the cow-shed. Then he covered the wound on his right side with his left hand, so no one could see it.

He had had enough. Leprosy and he was starving, eyesore, but still looking up, while the friars were squabbling.

A man in Rome told me that a monkey climbed down a wall holding an infant in his arms and in remembrance there is a statue of the Madonna on the very rooftop where he began his descent.

*

In 1950 Roberto Rossellini made a movie based on the life of Francis called *The Little Flowers of St. Francis.*
It included flowers pulled from bushes, flowers as white and immaculate as Swann's own hawthorne.

Rossellini's ethic in film-making was Franciscan: to use little money, shoot spontaneously and edit not much.

Like the "first word, best word" school of poetry, Rossellini mistrusted the process of refinement and treated his films as some might treat their notebooks, or first drafts.

This method worked for a number of reasons. He was already a director comfortable with his work, and he knew what the limits of his subject were. Complexity of character was not an issue.

Rossellini, a man who loved women, was a communist for a time and a Catholic as a child. He was obsessed by the Second World War and Italy's behavior under Mussolini. He hoped St. Francis, as a radical and fully enlightened subject, might redeem the shameful failure of his country to mobilize against Hitler.

"The perfect present for poetry loving friends..."

BUY A GIFT MEMBERSHIP FOR CHRISTMAS

POETRY SOCIETY MEMBERS RECEIVE:

- *Poetry Review* – Britain's premier poetry magazine with the best contemporary poetry, reviews and essays every quarter
- *Poetry News* – exclusive members' newspaper, with members' poems, prizes, features and news
- Discounts at events, readings and bookshops
- Monthly e-bulletins with exciting offers and prize drawers
- Free second entry to the National Poetry Competition

and much, much more...

MEMBERSHIP (inc *Poetry Review*)
UK from £40 • Europe from £50 • RoW from £55

Contact membership@poetrysociety.org.uk • 020 7420 9881

THE POETRY SOCIETY

www.poetrysociety.org.uk

The Further Reach

MAITREYABANDHU

Ah, but a man's reach should exceed his grasp
or what's a heaven for?
> – Robert Browning, 'Andrea del Sarto'

We are creatures at once vexed and consoled by summons of a
freedom just out of reach.
> – George Steiner, *Real Presences*[1]

I'd taken Mimi Khalvati a short lyric to look at. I'd been fortunate enough to be awarded a place on the Arvon/Jerwood mentoring scheme with Mimi as my mentor. It was one of those poems where I'd been 'given' the first line. I was on holiday in New Zealand when it happened: "The sea was grey but the island was missing". And like so many newcomers to the art, I was pretty happy with it, and with the sixteen lines that followed. I thought Mimi might delete a comma here, suggest a different word there – the kinds of thing newcomers like me think 'working on a poem' means. She held it to the light as if to see a watermark, then said it wanted to be longer; that it was to do with a sense of timelessness. But that doesn't do her justice. What she actually did was *inhabit* the poem... not the poem I'd written but the poem my poem was trying to be. Instead of the tedium of explanation, she acted out my poem's shape – its tone of voice, its syntax. Her description of the poem-to-be, the potential for a poem in what I'd written, was gestural as much as anything – a word thrown over her shoulder, a few words, "The sun rose...then it set...at night the moon..." It communicated everything I needed to know.

I started working on it a few days later. But where to start? I'd said everything I wanted to say. There *was* nothing else. But I remembered Mimi's gestures, her tone of voice. And I remembered the words, "The sun rose" (not very promising words). So I typed them in: "The sun rose". And that's when it happened. The poem opened up, or rather something new, something beyond the poem and my holiday and what I thought about the coast – the gulls, the sea – entered into the poem. It was like Tracy Island in

---

1. *Real Presences.* The University of Chicago Press, p. 153.

Thunderbirds. The beach slid apart, the palm trees pivoted. Thunderbird 2 rose out of the ground.

I want to explore the experience of something new entering a poem. I want to do this from a Buddhist point of view. And I'm hoping that you, the reader, will have read my article 'The Provenance of Pleasure' (*Poetry Review*, Spring 2011), because I want to build on that here. Buddhism is trying to point us to direct experience. Its concern is to help us see what is valuable and then to live out that value in every aspect of our life. It is not primarily preoccupied with belief or theory; it has no 'mania for explanation' – though it can certainly look like it has! Buddhism needs to be approached in the same spirit that Mimi read my poem: suggestively, sympathetically, trying to see what's being got at, what *shape* is being articulated below the surface clumsiness of words.

My experience of writing that day is difficult to pin down. There was the feeling of something entering the poem from beyond me, coupled with a sense of hitting my stride, finding my feet, of the whole thing taking off. I experienced a new fluency and confidence, as well as a strong but unselfconscious interest. Time seemed to stop. My usual experience of myself – my identity, my individuality – seemed temporarily suspended. It's the sort of experience anyone writing poems is searching for: as if you're the vessel of poetry, not its author. And I'm not making claims for my own writing here. I'm not suggesting I'm especially in touch with the muse; I'm just trying to get at experiences we all have to one degree or another.

I want to call these experiences 'imagination'. I want to make a case for imagination as an intrinsic faculty that can be recognised, enriched and matured so that it becomes the decisive force of our life. I want to make a case for imagination in the Coleridgian sense – a faculty that unites and transcends reason and emotion and points us toward a deeper understanding of life beyond the limitations of the rational. I want to suggest that imagination has within it something that goes beyond our fixed identity and narrow certainties.

To do that, we'll need to hold words lightly. 'Imagination' has become a trivial word; little remains of what Blake and Coleridge meant by it. Modern western culture has mostly lost touch with the depth and importance of imagination; it's just another part of the entertainment industry. At the same time 'imagination' can also be used to glorify the irrational or as another weapon in the war against reasoned thought. The word 'spiritual' is also problematic – it often dignifies exoticism, sentimentality or mere woolly-headedness. So I want to try to explore what actually *happens* when imagination takes flight: words can only approximate to that.

Coleridge contrasts imagination with "fancy". Fancy, to use the words of Iggy Pop, is just "The same old thing in brand new drag" – the usual contents of experiences but put together in unusual, arbitrary combinations. It has all the impact of novelty, and is typified by the kind of poetry that juxtaposes a zebra, a hypodermic syringe, an orange and a stick of underarm deodorant. With fancy, nothing *more* is being got at – there is no inner cohesion, no imaginative unity of meaning, no deeper perception: it is novelty for novelty's sake. In today's poetry climate – the sheer number of writers jostling for the attention of so few readers, the burgeoning business of 'creative writing', the need for a quick fix in all things – it can feel especially tempting to write from fancy rather than mine for imagination (which is far more difficult to extract). In a market-driven world, the quirky, the strange and the 'original', seem the most likely 'product' to catch the reader's eye. Essentially, with fancy nothing genuinely *new*, nothing from outside the poet's conscious identity, has entered the poem – it's the poet in outlandish costume and funny hat, but it's still the same old poet.[2]

For a poem to be the work of imagination (rather than fancy), it must go at least a little way beyond the poet's present ability and skill. In any genuinely imaginative experience, something *unwilled* enters – something strange and yet familiar. A modern poem that exemplifies this animating intrusion, this shifting of the light, is Ted Hughes's 'The Thought-Fox':

> I imagine this midnight moment's forest:
> Something else is alive
> Beside the clock's loneliness
> And this blank page where my fingers move.

This "something", this Thought-Fox, comes from outside, from animist nature. It is felt to be nearer than the stars: so it isn't God or the angelic hierarchy. It's "deeper within darkness" – feral, silent, making "neat prints" in the snow – but also brilliant and concentrated; its eyes "A widening deepening greenness". The Thought-Fox has no interest in the poet: it is "Coming about its own business". It's an atmosphere; a presence: "with the

---

2. 'Fancy' is a kind of mechanical way of seeing the world: rearranging the contents of experience into new combinations without changing their fundamental character. It is the poetry of *prapañca* (metal proliferation, 'spreading out'). *Prapañchic* poetry – based on the mind's speculative wanderings – can be extremely sophisticated, even virtuosic, but it never *moves*; it never addresses the whole person.

sudden sharp hot stink of fox / It enters the dark hole of the head". Then comes the evocative final line where poet-writing and fox-walking are unified into a single image: "The page is printed." Hughes's celebrated poem enacts the animating experience of imagination – of something uncanny entering the poem and turning unjustified lines of prose into poetic utterance. We could call this the 'metaphor of otherness': something beyond the individual has entered the work. And note, for Hughes at least, this is not a *literal* other – Deity or angel. It is experienced as something coming from the natural world (I'll come back to that), which enters the poet's mind and thereby writes the poem.

The 'metaphor of otherness' helps us understand another facet of imagination. The arrival of the Thought-Fox – the new, the unwilled – enters the poem and touches it with "immortal fire" (to use Auden's phrase). There is a sense in which the object is *alive* – whether that object is a sculpture, a piece of music or a poem. Imagination spontaneously selects sights, sounds, thoughts, images and so forth, and organises them into pleasurable formal relations[3] that draw out their deeper significance, expressing fundamental truths beyond the machinery of conceptual thought.[4] In other words, imagination selects and *transforms* the data of experience, giving it new depth and purchase. Hughes's poem selects the absence of stars, a clock, loneliness, a fox's cold nose, snow, the movement of a hand across a page, midnight, a bad smell, and so on... to illuminate meanings that lie beyond the reach of words. The poem becomes a symbol for something beyond the poem. That 'something beyond' is experienced as taking up residence within the poem, without at the same time being reducible to it. Although all achieved poems can be paraphrased, their significance can only be

---

3. In *The Provenance of Pleasure* (PR 101:1), I tried to show how hedonic sensations (Skt. *Vedanā*) – the feeling of getting into a bath or receiving a critical email – are pleasant, unpleasant or neutral; and that these sensations can be worldly (*sāmisa*) or unworldly (*nirāmisa*). I should have added that reading poetry can be both positive (*nirāmisa*) and *painful*. The work of Owen and Celan come to mind, or Auden's utterly comfortless poem 'The Shield of Achilles'. It follows that poems can also be pleasurable and *worldly* (*sāmisa*), with no deeper purchase on life. This 'worldliness' is nothing to do with subject matter (religious poems can be worldly) but with whether or not imagination has taken flight.

4. Buddhism distinguishes between two kinds of thought: integrated thought founded on direct experience – including physical sensations – and alienated thought (Skt. *Prapañca*). *Prapañca* is thinking in a vacuum; it is thought out of touch with direct experience, especially sensations of the body. Imagination is the faculty that replaces *prapañca* in deepened experience. Imagination includes integrated thought, but it suspends rumination (*prapañca*), at least temporarily. Interestingly, imagination has some of the attributes of *prapañca* – like *prapañca* it connects one thing with another, sometimes at a great distance, in order to make sense of experience (metaphor). But it does this in a wholly positive and integrated way, unifying the contents of experience into an ever-greater whole. (See *The Provenance of Pleasure*.)

apprehended through the particular words, images and syntactical manoeuvres within the poem. The meaning of King Lear isn't 'Foolish King learns genuine humanity by losing everything'. It's not the moral of a fairy story. It's the mastering presence felt to reside within the work.

The transformative power of imagination works in a second way: the object's aliveness seems to transform *us*. Rilke's last line from 'Archaic Torso of Apollo' is paradigmatic: "[...] for here there is no place / that does not see you. You must change your life." It is as though something of the aliveness of the subject has been invested in the object. As though something of Hughes's uplifted imagination has impregnated itself into the poem and can be experienced directly by the attentive reader. Reader and poet, subject and object, seem to step closer to one another and interact in a new vital way, overthrowing the usual categories of perception. We could call this 'inter-subjectivity': the poem or sculpture is felt to be another experiencing subject rather than an inanimate object. This is why (at best) we read poems, go to galleries or attend concerts. And the theological impulse is a natural one – it describes or seems to describe certain heightened experiences we have while reading Keats or listening to Bach.

Of course another way of talking about imagination is in terms of the 'metaphor of discovery'. Good writing, as any poet knows, is a process of discovery. You are trying to fathom something you can't quite think, can't quite feel. You have hunches and clues, but there are plenty of red herrings. When we manage to write a successful poem there's often the feeling that all along, beneath the effort of drafting and re-drafting, some greater thought, some more unified perception was trying to be expressed. You – the person who sits and writes and worries about publication – you could not have written it. This is what Keats was getting at in that famous letter to his brother: "Negative Capability, that is when a man is capable of being in uncertainties, Mysteries, doubts without any irritable reaching after fact & reason".[5]

Jo Shapcott's poem 'Composition' (from her 2010 collection *Of Mutability*) is a poem about discovering a poem, just as Ted Hughes's poem is

---

5. What happens when we try to solve a problem – to get the poem to work or clinch the last line – is that the mind automatically narrows to exclude experiences that don't seem to offer a solution. In one study, researchers stopped students in the campus grounds and, holding a campus map, asked them if they could give directions to a nearby building. Halfway through the encounter, two men carrying a door passed between the questioner and the student, during which time the questioner was replaced with a different person – different age, different sex, different clothes. The first time this study was undertaken only 47% of people noticed. The second time only 33%. Somehow in a poem, we are trying to negotiate intentionality (will) without losing imaginative and experiential breadth. We need Keats's 'Negative Capability' to stop our mind fixating on limited and self-conscious 'solutions'.

a poem about the 'otherness' of true imagination. In fact, in this context, Shapcott's poem looks like a serio-comic commentary on Hughes's 'Thought-Fox':

> And I sat among dust motes, my pencil
> (blue) sounding loud on the page, and
> a blast of sun hit a puddle [...]

Shapcott's poem is wonderfully deft:

> then eternity trembled
> and my fingers smelled of garlic from before
>
> and the window was smeary, the tea cups
> wanted washing and the Gulf Stream
> was slowing and O my hips
>
> ached from sitting.

The serio-comic aspect of Shapcott's writing brings out another dimension of the imaginal: playfulness. Imagination is not directed at any kind of worldly utility or function (Auden's "Poetry makes nothing happen"). At best it is a completely spontaneous play. This is not to say imagination doesn't achieve anything, rather that in our "sudden elevations of mind", as Samuel Johnson called them, the polarities of success and failure are overthrown (if only temporarily). The tendency of imagination is to overcome polarities. For instance, imagination unifies and transcends the distinction we often make between 'serious' and 'not serious'. Shapcott's poem demonstrates that we can't be serious in the *wrong* way – portentous, over-earnest, highfaluting – if we want to be serious in the *right* way:

> and hurricanoes whirled and hissed,
> my nose itched, my ears hurt,
> and then there was this.

A related point is that imagination often comes into play unexpectedly: it comes in sideward, when you least expect it, when you're doing something else, such as trying to be profound or (horror-upon-horror) original.

There are two more aspects of imagination I want to draw out before I explore what the experience of imagination might *mean* – let's call them the 'metaphor of unity' and the 'metaphor of ascent'. Any genuinely imaginative experience is characterised by a deeper sense of unity – as if the poem was "just one word" as Don Paterson put it. Imagination unifies the contents of experience by discovering something within them, some underlying meaning or significance, inaccessible to ordinary consciousness. Part of the experience of aliveness in a poem, of inter-subjectivity, is this sense of internal ramification, of every part of the poem knowing about every other part of the poem (Eliot's "The complete consort dancing together"). A poem can mean many things, even apparently contradictory things, without disrupting the poem's internal cohesion and harmony. This is what really good writing is aiming at; and it's a thousand times more difficult than finding striking metaphors or gorgeous syntax.[6]

Imagination also unifies the *poet* – better still imagination *is* the unified consciousness of the poet. It draws together his or her cognitive, emotional and volitional powers, blends them with subtlised and refined sensation, including physical sensation, and melds them together into a single act of awareness. This sense of unification is deeply satisfying.[7] Until then it's like you'd been driving with the handbrake on.

Finally: 'the metaphor of ascent'. Imagination acts as an intermediary between our everyday, run-of-the mill self – the self that sits down at the computer with a cup of tea – and something (let's call it 'X' for the time being) that transcends the self. The images that imagination selects partake in both the world and something beyond the world. They seem to draw something *up* from the poet – from the ordinary contents of everyday life – and draw something *down* from beyond the poet. It is a traditional practice in Buddhism to imagine the Buddha and the qualities of Enlightenment so as to experience something of these qualities for yourself. And it's clearly *you* doing it – trying to keep the Buddha in mind, coming back to him whenever you get distracted. But sometimes, the image takes on a life of its own, seems illumined by an order of reality that lies beyond the figure and yet manifests

---

6. Again, the theological impulse is a natural one: we end up playing God. We can't help wanting to get everything in, trying to uncover the underlying interrelatedness of everything. Jo Shapcott's 'Composition' wants to unify global warming, eternity, her fingers smelling of garlic, and so on... into a single harmonious whole. This desire to keep widening the net of poetry is one of the challenges of contemporary poetry – how can we write about CNN News, iPhones and adverts and still create a poem? In practice, it's not always clear if our writing is the product of fancy or imagination. The test is how it leaves us (and hopefully our readers) feeling at the end – enhanced and unified or enervated and distracted?

7. The unification of our psychophysical energy – 'the whole person, wholly attending' – is the first goal of Buddhist meditation. It is a deeply pleasurable and meaningful experience.

through it – like stained glass illumined by the sun. The best in poetry, the best in the arts, has something analogous to this illumined quality. And it's signalled by a release of energy: by our imagination – emotion, thought, perception, sensation – being unified into a single whole then set alight.[8]

Imagination has within it this impulse to ascend to higher and higher levels of meaning and 'revelation'. It is this ascending nature that accounts for the best of the best – writers, artists, composers etc., for whom the word 'genius' is needed to make a distinction between capacity, even great capacity, and imaginative gifts of quite another order. As the imagination ascends, there is a greater and greater sense of unity, discovery, aliveness and spontaneity. This is coupled with a deepening sense of pleasure as well as an intensifying revelation of meaning – a powerful and transforming satisfaction that is both aesthetic and cognitive.

There is a connection between these heights of imagination and our own work. In writing my poem under Mimi's guidance, I caught a whiff of imagination's sudden uplift. It seemed to have its own syntax, its own shape and atmosphere, even its own presiding deity (Elizabeth Bishop). I couldn't have 'thought it up'. In the writing Mimi nudged me towards, I experienced some of the characteristic attributes of imagination: otherness, aliveness, discovery, playfulness, ease and meaning – coupled with the sense of suspended rumination (*prapañca*), the feeling that some deeper truth was being unearthed.

*

Imagination is the mind functioning at its most integrated and penetrating. It is the entirety of the person – reason, emotion, volition, and sensation – blended into complete action. It can be like Caravaggio's 'St Matthew and the Angel' in the Cappella Contarelli in Rome – a disruptive intrusion breaking into the saint's limited human consciousness and writing the Gospel: "The page is printed". But it can also be that fleeting sense of uplift – the sentence found, the word given. As with all valuable experiences, our instinct will be to reify it into a *literal* other (a "real presence" as George Steiner puts it, i.e. God) or to deny it (Steiner's "real absence"). Both are explanations after the

---

8. Take Rilke's 'Sonnets to Orpheus' as an example. In a letter to Xaver von Moos in April 1923, Rilke says the sonnets "are perhaps the most mysterious, most enigmatic dictation I have ever endured and achieved; the whole of the first part [twenty six poems] was written in a single breathless obedience, between 2nd and 5th February 1922, without one word being in doubt or having to be changed".

fact. They are trying to get at something: the sense of finding your form or the feeling of being guided by something beyond yourself. Our instinct, once the experience has waned, is to reduce it to one side of the equation. Which side we fall will depend on our family background, our religious upbringing (or lack of it), our views and cultural affiliations. Faced with the ungraspable mystery of experience – and our deep sense of insecurity in the face of that – we will tend to fix the mystery into the shape of God or into an unaided, ordinary human being. These two tendencies (really they are deep pre-conscious beliefs) are what Buddhism calls 'eternalism' and 'nihilism'. Buddhism is trying to suggest a third alternative – beyond the polarisations of religion and science, beyond the Pope and Richard Dawkins.[9]

But can we discover a theory of imagination that doesn't fall into *Yes* (God/eternalism) or *No* (materialism/nihilism)? The Buddha himself was 'metaphysically reticent'. He sought to avoid all speculative thinking. He would have said that questions concerning the existence or non-existence of God, the ontological status of objects, the true nature of space and time, are questions without answers, or rather questions that cannot be answered within the either-or of rational thought. Our instinct, backed up by the structure of language, is to say that something either exists (can be weighed, photographed or touched) or doesn't exist. The Buddha was essentially pragmatic. He taught people how to understand and then change their mind – so they could find the truth for themselves, beyond all conceptual designations.

However, the Buddha *did* sometimes talk about the nature of reality. His most important formulation is *Pratītya-samutpāda* – 'conditioned co-production' or 'conditioned arising'. It is not a theory about things; it is a description of what we see when we look at life deeply. It is the 'middle way' beyond the 'extremes' (as the Buddha called them) of eternalism and nihilism. It avoids eternalism by stressing that all things arise in dependence on conditions. There are no fixed essences such as 'self' or 'soul' and no really existing entities such as 'God'.[10] All things are dependently arising and

---

9. Eternalism and nihilism are both beliefs – in the sense of deep unconscious assumptions, beyond the scope of conscious opinion or theory. The Buddha called them 'unhelpful views' (Skt. *micchā-diṭṭhis*) meaning that, after a certain point, they limit spiritual growth. One characteristic of materialism/nihilism is the tendency to mistake beliefs for facts. We could say nihilism is a belief that has forgotten it's a belief.

10. The Buddha urged his disciples to stay close to the contours of experience rather than involve themselves in speculative views about the nature of existence. Although Buddhism does not believe in a creator God, it might be more accurate to say that God is not a language Buddhists use or find helpful. The actual *experiences* that are being labelled divine may well have a lot in common with Buddhism.

ceasing. All things are impermanent. But *Pratītya-samutpāda* avoids nihilism by asserting the possibility of a path of self-transcendence.

Pratītya-samutpāda is "the general principle of ordered relationship between conditions and their effects".[11] It is saying that when we look at our experience, we see various kinds of regularities. The Buddha talked about a whole range of interacting conditioned processes, but he never clearly classified them: we need to look to Buddhaghosa, the fifth century Theravādin Buddhist scholar, for that. He grouped all conditioned relationships into five different orders of regularities called the five *niyāmas*. Put simply, the first three *niyāmas* are those regularities discerned by the sciences: regularities that govern inorganic matter; organic life; and simple consciousness, including instincts. So for instance, we live in a world governed by the laws of gravity, by the processes of photosynthesis, and by the migratory instincts of swallows.

Buddhaghosa then goes on to innumerate two *further* levels of conditioned processes. Firstly, a patterning or regularity that governs the relationship between self-conscious agents (you and me) and the effects of our actions (*kamma-niyāma*); and secondly the regularities governing the transcending, progressive potential within human consciousness, culminating in the emergence of a Buddha (*dhamma-niyāma*). Leaving aside the *dhamma-niyāma* for a moment, *kamma-niyāma* processes are those laws that govern ethical life. They emphasise the central importance of *our states of mind* – especially the intentions that underpin our actions. So, if I act from awareness and unselfish intentions I will, generally speaking, experience pleasant feedback from my environment; I will be more liable to feel inner satisfaction, and my experience will feel enriched and deepened. Conversely, if I act from unawareness or selfish intentions, I will generally speaking, experience *un*pleasant feedback from my environment; I will feel discontent and unhappy, and my experience will feel narrow and cramped. *Kamma-niyāma* is saying the universe is structured in such a way that the consequences of a conscious action are appropriate to the volitional impulse behind the action. *Kamma-niyāma* processes mean that our states of mind broadly condition the kind of world we experience.[12] *Pratītya-samutpāda* is saying this is a law, like the law of gravity or thermodynamics – you can know

---

11. I am very much indebted to two articles by Urgyen Sangharakshita (founder of the Triratna Buddhist Order) and Dharmachari Subhuti: *Revering and Relying upon the Dharma* and *Re-imagining the Buddha* (www.sangharakshita.org).

12. The Pali word *kamma* is better known in the west by its Sanskrit equivalent, karma. Karma simply means 'action', while *karma vipāka* means the fruit or consequence of action. Unfortunately this 'law of karma' has been misunderstood to mean that whatever happens to you is because of

about it or not, believe in it or not, but it's operating just the same.

It is this law of *kamma-niyāma* that governs our "sudden elevations of mind". In creative experience we are (without being self-conscious about it) in positive states of mind: we are concentrated, un-distracted, content. Our experience has greater depth and lustre; feels brighter and clearer; is more malleable, responsive, enriched and uplifted. We feel that sense of integration, even inspiration. We don't especially *want* something or *not want* something – for a while at least we're free of all that. In other words, our experience is emerging in new, more subtle and refined ways. All this is happening under the law of *kamma-niyāma*: positive states of mind fashion consciousness into new forms – forms we could call 'imagination'.

And sometimes our imagination is so enriched, we seem to lose all sense of ourselves; we seem to step beyond the limits of 'me'. At these moments something beyond the self irrupts into the self. It is perfectly natural, like Hughes' 'Thought-Fox'. It is not a really existent other (God): "The window is starless still". It is "Coming about its own business": *it cannot be willed*. Yet it completely transcends our usual self-consciousness, even the elevated sense of ourselves in imaginative experience. We cannot but experience it as coming from beyond the self. We have made the effort to write, to find our way into concentrated absorption, but then something goes beyond our "stitching and unstitching" (as Yeats put it) – some new force takes over: "The page is printed." These are the *dhamma-niyāma* processes at work, or at least the outer edges of them irrupting into "the small house of our cautionary being".[13] They are felt as a will that goes beyond our will, a gravitational pull that draws us into a new and larger orbit.

*

Imagination is the mind working under the laws of *kamma-niyāma*. As such, it always takes us a little way beyond ourselves into a richer dimension of experience. It is not the sole domain of artists and poets, though it's typically discussed in reference to them. It informs the best of science and mathematics, the best in human endeavour. It is essentially ethical, a going beyond self-clinging. The main difference between spiritual life and the path of the poet is that the first is a self-conscious mind-training, while the second

something you have done in the past. The five *niyāmas* explicitly reject that idea, as did the Buddha himself: any of the five *niyāmas*, singly or combination, could be involved. We could think of this widespread misunderstanding as the 'Glen Hoddle Error'.
13. Steiner, *Real Presences*, p. 143.

is more ad hoc – breakthroughs into a new modes of consciousness are accessible to the poet *within* the work, but they fall away outside it. (This accounts for the famous double life of poets – how they can oscillate between god-like creation and animal-like behaviour.) Imagination's sudden uplifts are sustained by the laws of *kamma-niyāma*. But as soon as we *want* something, as soon as the usual 'me' takes over – tries to be 'poetic' or clever or coarse – we're back on the stony ground of self. Egoism in poetry, as in any other field of life, is always predictable, doomed to repetition and banality or destined to tedious self-aggrandisement. We're back to Coleridge's 'fancy', to the poetry of *prapañca* – mere connoisseurship, empty virtuosity.

Without some glimmer of the *dhamma-niyāma* order of conditionality manifesting within our enriched and uplifted experience, our imagination will falter; we will regress back to habitual, repetitive selfhood. Without some sense of this unwilled, self-transcending reality, our work as a poet will sink to the level of refined egotism – and refined egotism has the tendency to calcify into preciousness, self-absorption or snobbery. Without some contact with *dhamma-niyāma* conditionality – some glimpse of a glimpse at least – our imagination will be limited and immature. We need trust in, and some experience of, the *dhamma-niyāma* processes at work in reality. The Sanskrit word for this trust is *śraddhā*. *Śraddhā* is faith in the ascending imagination – its capacity for direct apprehension, its ability to see life whole and in so doing become whole ourselves.

In our best readings of the best work, we sometimes feel intimations of an order of reality that completely transcends us, as if the work took us to the very edges of form and pointed beyond itself to some formless, timeless mystery. For Buddhists, the Buddha is the embodiment of that mystery – for complete self-transcendence, beyond the dualities of 'self' and 'world', 'you' and 'me', 'time' and 'timelessness'. And transcendence is not vacancy or negation, but the complete fulfilment of everything – a breaking down of all boundaries. This mystery, this *dhamma-niyāma* aspect of conditionality, finds its roots here and now, in every moment we go beyond ourselves, whether by acts of imagination or in our everyday kindness and generosity. *Śraddhā* or 'confidence-trust' is trust in the third alternative, beyond the affirmations of divinity or the negations of scientific materialism. It is the intuition *in* the self for something *beyond* the self – a mirror in the "rag and bone shop of the heart" reflecting the sky.

Maitreyabandhu lives and works at the London Buddhist Centre and has been ordained into the Triratna Buddhist Order for twenty years. His pamphlet, *The Band*, was published by Smith/Doorstop in May 2011.

Poetry As Technology

GWYNETH LEWIS

A few years ago, I heard a poet pronounce that poetry is everything that technology is not. The idea was that poetry is non-polluting (debatable), carbon neutral (not necessarily), fixed in a pre-lapsarian area of the brain (definitely not). This line seems to me to be absurd. Language was one of man's earliest technologies. It's younger than the pebble chopper and the stitching of textiles together, as far as we can tell (language leaves no fossils). One of the reasons for the demise of the Neanderthal is thought to be that limitations in the flexibility of his larynx prevented rapid tongue movements. *Homo sapiens* was able to form a wider range of clear sounds. These allowed him to form complex sentences and so to trade his tools, laying the foundations of human society which extended beyond the Neanderthal's small family units. So begins the complex intercourse between objects and their symbolic representations.

I'm discussing poetry now because it's the extreme sport of language, but what I say applies to all formal uses of language, however diffuse. From the moment we begin to use words to call to our mother and tell her what we want, we're beginning to create an avatar. If you like, Helen of Troy splits into two – imago, and flesh-and-blood woman. I view poetry as having been from the earliest times a form of virtual reality. Like computer games, it's addictive. W.H. Auden used to say that the only two labour-saving devices available to the writer were coffee and cigarettes. Now we have a wider range of flavours to choose from the psychopharmacy – from SSRIs to Ritalin – to act on our neurotransmitters. However, this misses the basic point about poetry, which is that it is, in itself, a mood-altering technology. Research has shown that, in rats, rhythmic activity releases dopamine into the brain. It's rumoured that oxydosin, the substance that precipitates orgasm and the jetting of breast milk, has been dubbed the molecule that appreciates metaphor, so take care where you sit in the next poetry reading.

If this is true, it's no wonder that Welsh poets have a reputation as heavy drinkers. I've recently been reading the fourteenth-century poet Dafydd ap Gwilym. He writes in the most fiendishly complex metrical system I've ever come across – the *cynghanedd*. You've heard its effects in English on Gerard Manley Hopkins. If blank verse is skimmed milk, then poetry written in *cynghanedd* is clotted cream. Take these lines (here even a native speaker has to swallow her spittle and approach with care). This is an ode to the wind:

> Nythod ddwyn, cyd nithud ddail
> Ni'th dditia neb, ni'th etail
> Na llu rhugl, na llaw rhaglaw,
> Na llafn glas na llif nag law.

For the poet's nervous system, this isn't smoking a joint, it's mainlining heroin.

It's tempting to think of the body itself as a machine for which we haven't got the manual. This won't do, because it's an organic entity. However permissive we like to be with regard to technology, we're curiously conservative in our attitude to the body, as if it had exact boundaries. In truth, it's always been a culturally mediated entity. Try to locate it and you'll find it's a concertina, a stream which suddenly flows underground. Without medical intervention, many of us would not be here and most would be without their teeth. It's no accident, I feel, that one of the dominant pathologies of our time is that of body dysmorphia. We have good reason to be unsure where our bodies end and another begins. It's the anxiety of a time when our reach is being extended way beyond the local. Recently I was at the Worlds Literature Festival 2011 in Norwich and heard somebody ask: "What happens if we take the body out of it?" That's not an option, though. The real question is: what happens when we see how far the mind can extend through our new body, the internet? This social networking isn't a replacement of the old way of being human together, but an addition to it.

Sherry Turkle has written about the relationship between the computer and the human spirit. She says:

> We asked of the Wild Child to speak to us about our relationship to nature. But of the computer we ask more. We ask not just about where we stand in nature, but about where we stand in the world of the artifact.

In her novel, *The Keep*, Jennifer Egan describes a character who's suffering from internet withdrawal symptoms. When he finally connects and relaxes into two simultaneous conversations, he realizes that

> he was at home right at that moment. Not in Washington Square [...] not in Peru, where he'd never been in his life, but *both places at once*.

So, here's the surfer, constantly being remade by the changing times, locations and characters through which his search history takes him. He is the living metaphor, a breathing translation. Not writing metaphors, he is the thing itself. This is, I believe, a significant new development in the nature of symbolic language. More than ever before, it's brought metaphor right into the body, which doesn't always understand the distinction between a symbol and the reality to which it refers.

So, what does it mean, this collapse in the distinction between phenomenon and symbol, progenitor and avatar; this endless chain of clones with no mother for Dolly the sheep to revere as ancestor? These Big Bangs happening everywhere, at once? The fear is: chaos. Being overwhelmed by degraded information. I ask myself what Virginia Woolf would have thought of the internet. I think she would have approved. John Milton would have been on the side of the wiki leakers, on the grounds that it isn't information itself that corrupts, but the uses to which it's put. He would have tussled with it but come out, I believe, on the side of free speech, however uncomfortable its current forms make us feel.

Dmitri Kuzmin, a participant at Worlds 2011, asked how would it be if we took being *influenced by everything at once* as a source? The internet and its games are nothing more than the most vivid picture we have so far of the collective unconscious. Joseph Brodsky always taught that the poet's job is to serve language. He was completely unfazed by what other people called its degradations because he had faith in *logos*, that principle of sense which precedes our tidy verbal structures. *Logos* comes from the word for laying sticks together. Note: not making a model of the *Cutty Sark*, but just laying them alongside each other. We're meant to *make the connections* ourselves.

The Worlds conference was devoted to the theme of influence. Professor Jon Cook asked, "Can we do without the teacher?" I want to lay issues of teaching creative writing aside for one moment and ask what happens if you get rid of our teachers, *words*? What's left of a poem when you've got rid of all its translatable elements – its vocabulary, metaphysics, even its silences? What if we catch what its so-called spirit? What Maureen Freely has described as the crucial "unspeakable, unstable place"? The pre-linguistic medium of which we're mostly unaware but which is our ultimate context? What if there's a source behind all the noise, and we're all moving closer to it collectively?

Although religion was not part of the conference's explicit subject I was struck by how religious language rose to the surface of many discussions. This has made me wonder if we're not groping towards a territory of post-institutional religion in contemporary culture. Now I'm talking much more broadly than about art or even formal education. The new digital media is pushing us to become our own teachers and the main issue is talent – not exceptional individual aptitudes, but the ability of every person to grow beyond him or herself – in partnership with that non-transcendental inhuman force which American poet Joyelle McSweeney identifies, in her book *The Necropastoral,* as the inhuman element in technology. Now we're upstream from ethics because we're in the creative flow itself, where the rules inside the poem and those outside aren't different as they are down here and (I'm invoking, as I have to, Emily Dickinson: the great untranslatable resister, believer in the cloud of the future) the only safe Master is the imaginary one we kill and what rises thereafter.

I was commissioned recently by BBC Radio 3's *The Verb* to write a poem about anthologies. Once, as I was wandering in the backstreets of Bologna, I noticed a gym called Palaestra di Poeti. The idea of Emily Dickinson working a bench press was irresistible. In my anthology gym, a potential client is shown around the facilities by a sales person, who is the speaker. We meet W.H. Auden on the cross-trainer; Dylan Thomas's doing zumba. The tour's interrupted by the hi-fi system:

> "Let me turn
> The music down. Ted Hughes has found the knob,
> Likes heavy metal as he's pumping iron –
> He's muscle-bound, and been at war
> With the Brontë sisters who demand
> Glam rock for spinning. There. Can't go wrong
> With Gloria Gaynor."

And so on. Such an image is fun but can't offer an image of the new ways in which we're learning to influence each other online. So I wrote another (spot the echo of Lowell):

The Fountain

> With a hiss it stutters, startling sparrows and children,
> Sloshes its teeth, spurts out a song
> In arcs and droplets. An Alsatian bites
> A jet, gets little to drink, backs off
> Bowing, suspicious. I see a cathedral
> Which thinks in ropes. Sure, it's a con,
> This real illusion. It has no opinion
> On subjects. Though it plays

In peonies, fish scales, jellies it breaks
Without conscience. Like the Lord, it survives
Its own creatures. It's not outside
Me entirely so, when it falls,
Dropping the ball of itself (oh, the shame
Of believing!) it slops, soft clocks
Down drains, I ask "What's next?"
The dog sits waiting, stares
At a spigot. He whines, shifts haunches.
No, wait for it, focus, here it comes,
The bubble meniscus, the swelling. Now! Jump!

CHELTENHAM FESTIVAL 2011
THE NATIONAL POETRY COMPETITION WINNERS

In an event organised in partnership with
the Poetry Society, the 2010 winners of the
much-coveted National Poetry Competition:
Paul Adrian, **Jo Haslam** and **Matthew
Sweeney** join **Jo Shapcott** to read their
winning entries and a selection of new
work. Programmed by Jo Shapcott.

Friday 14 October, 12pm

IMPERIAL SQUARE
Main Hall, Garden Theatre
The Inkpot, The Studio
GL50 1QA

Tickets: £6 BOOKING CODE: L283

Box office: 01242 505444
www.cheltenhamfestivals.com

George Szirtes photo: Clarissa Upchurch

Bones Will Crow:
A Selection Of Contemporary Burmese Poetry

EDITED BY KO KO THETT AND JAMES BYRNE

The Burmese translations published here serve as the initial feature from an anthology project that has been in preparation since January 2009. Back then I was introduced to Vicky Bowman, former British Ambassador to Burma (2002-2006), and her husband, the artist Htein Lin. I was attempting to solicit a brief introduction to Burmese poetry to be published alongside new translations. Later that year Vicky and Htein Lin wrote a piece on 'Contemporary Burmese Poetry' for *The Wolf: 21* (http://www.wolf magazine.co.uk/21_burmese.php). Previously, my only real involvement with Burmese poetry was to publish two versions of poems by Saw Wai, undertaken by Niall McDevitt and Myint Swe. At the time of going to press Saw Wai was imprisoned in the notorious Insein prison near Rangoon for writing an apparently-slushy love poem entitled 'February 14th', which acrostically criticised "power mad" General Than Shwe, the former leader of Burma's ruling military junta. On each February 14th during Saw Wai's jail term hundreds of Valentine cards were posted through the door of the Burmese Embassy in London, and his poems were read by McDevitt with a bodhran drum for accompaniment. After English PEN protested against Saw Wai's imprisonment he was released after little more than two years: merciful by the standards of the *tatmadaw*, who have ruled Burma since declaring martial law in September 1988.

There has never been an anthology of contemporary Burmese poetry published outside Burma, which is odd considering the quality of work available. From pre-colonial Burma to the contemporary scene poetry has always been the most common form of literature. Inside Burma, the most significant anthologies published in the last ten years have been edited by Maung Tha Noe, a leading linguist and teacher of Burmese and international poetry, and Mya Zin, a prominent scholar. Maung Tha Noe's *Burmese Verse: A Selection* was published in Rangoon in 2008 and includes some of the most beloved poets of twentieth century Burmese poetry, such as Min Thu Win (1906-2004), Zawgyi (1907-1990) and Dagon Taya, now in his nineties.

As co-editors of *Bones Will Crow*, ko ko thett and I have made some difficult decisions concerning chronology, particularly when leaving out the aforementioned trio of poets. We decided to select explicitly from contemporary writers who exemplify the post-modern aesthetic that has, once again, extended the Burmese literary tradition. The poets in this feature, and the anthology as a whole, include the most significant poets from Burma who are writing today, such as Zeyar Lynn, who claims to be more interested in "poetry of the brain" than of the heart. This was a radical shift for Burmese poetry in the 1990s and Zeyar Lynn's approach, along with his translations of Ashbery, Bernstein, Szymborska and others new to the Burmese canon, has influenced poets from his own generation – like Khin Aung Aye and Moe Way – to move away from the traditional strictures of conventional form, and appreciate 'imported' forms like LANGUAGE-orientated poetry.

Zeyar Lynn (whose nickname is 'The Guru') has also influenced a new generation of Burmese women poets, like Pandora and Eaindra. Perhaps a reflection of prevailing misogynistic values, poetry in Burma has for too long been considered a man's sport, even a chance to woo women (or at least keep them as the object of poetry rather than its practitioner). Things are starting to change, in part because of the emergence of a poetry that derives from the intellect as much as from the passions, but also because publishing opportunities in Burma have changed. From their bases in Singapore, Pandora and Eaindra both publish poems on their blogs as much as in print magazines. In Burma itself, magazines are often heavily censored by the strong arm of the Ministry of Information, and Burmese poets on home soil have to be incredibly inventive for their work to be printed "pure" or unredacted. All poets have a pen-name, and there is a good deal of respect given for an original one (Thitsar Ni's roughly translates as 'Loyal Red'). However, many poets who are seen to be unsupportive or threatening to the junta are imprisoned on charges relating to their writing; thousands of artist 'dissidents' languish in the prisons of Burma, many on long sentences, suffering torture and living in inhumane conditions.

Though these may be inextricably linked, the message of our anthology is poetry over politics. In fact, none of the poets included in our selection of sixteen is actively or overtly political (Tin Moe being the exception. He died exiled in California in 2007). Saw Wai, currently the most publicised Burmese poet in the West because of his imprisonment and the events that preceded it, didn't make our final cut. It should be added that much of the poetry in the anthology could be seen as having nothing to do with internal

Burmese politics; from Pandora's 'Siege' to Zeyar Lynn's 'Beards', these are playfully iterative, high-imagination poems that prevail in spite of the oppressive tactics of the regime. Burma has been rightly criticised by the West for their human rights violations and rife political corruption. It is our hope that this selection offers an alternative view into Burma, one that enriches an understanding of the Burmese people through their deep literary traditions.

James Byrne

'Best Words in Translation'

POPESCU PRIZE EVENT AT THE 2011
ALDEBURGH POETRY FESTIVAL

Jane Draycott, one of this year's judges of the **Corneliu M Popescu Prize** for Poetry Translated from a European Language into English, celebrates the winner with a close reading of poems from the book.

She will also talk about the significance of the award and how she and fellow judge, Sasha Dugdale, reached their decision.

**Saturday 5 November
3-3.30pm**

PETER PEARS GALLERY
Aldeburgh, Suffolk
IP15 5AQ

FREE EVENT
www.thepoetrytrust.org

Photo: Jemimah Kuhfeld

MOE WAY has published more than ten collections and is a renowned publisher of The Eres press based in Rangoon. Alongside Zeyar Lynn (whom he has published with Khin Aung Aye), Moe Way has had a major impact on influencing postmodern poetic forms into the Burmese language.

If You Need To Piss, Go From The Other Room

With their mouths agape, the generation who are learning
The Korean War from history books
Some call it a challenge, others insanity
The piercing eye through the spectacles of the new salvation
Life in the downpour, in the square nail, line after line
Languages age, where do we go in traffic lanes
Riding Pegasus, strolling in the park canvas of a painting
Just like a nude statue, cigarette between our fingers
Hand in mouth, over the frames of reading glasses,
We oversight who we are
One after another
Falling down prostrate on the floor
In a fable knocking door-to-door
We manufacture our time
Let's run more and more advertisements
Manchester calendar, London bureau, Zurich desk, Vienna motorboat
Munich television, Moscow owl, New York chair
Osaka lampshade, Shanghai menu, Manila bed, Hong Kong pillow
Karachi comforter, Islamabad boots
Bangkok doormat, Doha Cup, Athens glass
Cairo bedspread, Sydney magazines
Anyone is welcome to the land of opportunity
Local life probing and pleasuring
Personal probing and personal worship
The classified file of pain opens on the crisis
The emergency propellers, the mechanical sigh as a last breath
The escape from history in the form of a long shadow
That man has been marked in red
Mingalaba, Welcome.

Translated by ko ko thett and James Byrne.

ZEYAR LYNN, who lives in Rangoon, is a poet, critic, writer, translator and language instructor. After 1990 he instigated a wider appreciation of postmodern and LANGUAGE poetry forms into Burmese and is seen by many as the most influential living poet in Burma. He has translated many Western poets into Burmese, including Donald Justice, John Ashbery and Charles Bernstein. In *Jacket2* he recently published an insightful prose piece on about the changing traditions of Burmese poetry. https://jacket2.org/commentary/language-oriented-poetry-myanmar.

The Ways Of The Beards

There is a hair 'The rhymeless of the world, unite!' in Marx's beard
Not growing a beard is existentialism, says Sartre
Helen's beard that has launched a thousand ships
Beards looking for a chin like words for a poem
Beard is the war-torn town of the chin in civil war
In the history of chin, beard is the defeated truth
The world burned down at Marilyn's beard
The mediocrities look elegant in media beards
Honoured with flexible beard awards
The beard of the capital decorated with electric lamps
O...the beard of dreams beyond form
The beard of the desert whirling at the end of my vision
A small red mole (still running) on the beard of social realism
We have emerged from the raincoat of the famous Bluebeard
Beard sobbing over my shoulder
This has happened, this has happened in Maria, this has happened in Beard
The news of the beard-ghost harrowing, yet scientifically proven
The youthful beard, the powerful storm
Just take care of your beard, language will take care of itself
Instead of writing poetry, why not just grow beard
Hey...beards of the world, let's get out of the lanugo
Into the scene of the beard on trial, many myths are said to be trafficked in
Probing at the word, the scar of the beard was found
'Don't let the flag fall, Fight until only your beard remains' say the

Bansai T-shirts

Stop press news 'The Beard has just called himself You'
The spokesbeard has been shaved temporarily
His beard was also silenced, so goes the story
Post-beardism and the history of histories scattered
The robbery of the three primary roots of the beard
'A Handbook to Mental Attitude Analysis' by Zen Beard
The morning of the humming beards in the cage
The virtuous beards who are no saints
Sisyphus rolling up the untrimmable beard of the gods
This is my favourite, this beard is my brand, she said
History will forgive my beard
To install electric power all over the country,
To establish beard power all over the land
Go away... you swine-head... you only love your beard
A beard is a beard is a beard, a rose is a rose is a rose
All of you belong to the beardless generation
God is playing dice with the beard.

Translated by ko ko thett

PANDORA was born in 1974 in Burma Delta. She currently writes from Singapore. As an English major at Rangoon University, she wrote poems and short stories for the campus magazines under several pen names, all of which she has now forgotten. She took a hiatus from writing when she came to Singapore to study in 2001 but bounced back into the scene in early 2007 as literary blogger *Pandora*. Since then her poems, essays and short stories have been seen in online Burmese journals and books and in printed media inside Burma.

The Scene Of The City Siege By The Daft

the daft have been hunting and gathering   they have climbed up the Great Wall   rambunctiously   they have shooed the Trojan Horse into the city when in Rome   they have built a bamboo Rome overnight   they do as the Romans do   the daft have back-stabbed Caesar during Antony's speech they have back-stabbed Brutus and clamoured Caesar Caesar Caesar exactly three times   the daft syndrome has to be cut down quickly or else one will become daft   the daft virus is airborne   the daft symptoms are feverishness and words flowing out of all the nine holes of the body   in twenty-four hours the patient becomes absolutely daft   the daft spit at the non-daft they lick them with their tongue   they bite them with their teeth   as the daft population grows the non-daft have to pretend to be daft   the way the daft look   the way the daft walk   the way the daft dress the way the daft work   the way the daft eat and sleep   the way the daft type   the daft fashion   the daft and non-daft are no longer distinguishable on the back of the horse Kannaka   the Prince Siddhartha had followed the ascetic path to shun the daft   he came back after the great awakening   he confronted the daft as the Buddha the emancipated   for the daft-thinking daft the *dhamma* preachers have had to downgrade their *dhamma* versions   the preachers die preaching   the daft have crucified Jesus Christ   the daft have assassinated Lady Diana   they have flattened the jungles in search of Marilyn Monroe and Michael Jackson they have snapped Tiger Woods' wood   they have scrambled for Socrates' poison cup   in unanimity the daft have decided to pronounce *'inanity' 'inanition'* they have decided to make do with cakes whenever

bread is not available   they have driven 'a man, his son and their mule'
out of the village   they have moved the Statue of Liberty to Baghdad
they have ordered an atom bomb from Einstein and they have made a
knife mark on the rib of their boat as the daft from all corners of the
planet are enjoying themselves in their merry-go-rounds   BOOOOM
'The sky is collapsing'   the deafening noise   the daft in uproar   the daft
in commotion the daft in chaos   the daft stampeding

Translated by ko ko thett.

C.K. Williams' 'Whacked' in a stunning limited edition

*To mark the occasion of the 2011 Poetry Society Annual Lecture, the Poetry Society
has produced a limited edition print of C.K. Williams' tour de force poem 'Whacked'*

Featuring striking woodcuts by the artist and former *Daily Telegraph* political
cartoonist Nicholas Garland, the edition was printed by Phil Abel of Hand &
Eye letterpress studio, London. Set in Plantin on a 200gsm Fabriano paper, the
print (folded to 297 x 200 mm) is
published in an edition of just 450,
making it the perfect souvenir and
gift this Christmas.

*Non-members: £12
Poetry Society members: £8
Signed copies are available at
no extra charge while stocks last.*

BUY ONLINE at http://www.poetrysociety.org.uk/shop/product/401/

THITSAR NI was born in Rangoon in 1946. His 1978 chapbook, *Myinsaing Archery*, was re-released in 2006 and is considered a watershed in contemporary Burmese poetry. He claims that he found a poet in himself after an accidental breakup. He is a Buddhist with no spouse, no bank account and no master. To him, a poem should be an anti-poem.

from Redundant Sentences

3.

After climbing down trees
We shake hands
We say Hey, Hi, Hello
Civilized as we are.
We have learned to draw a bowstring with an arrow
We have learned to be taxed
We have learned to use a white umbrella
Civilized as we are.
To turn skyscrapers into tombs
To turn the lights on when the sun sets
To wear a *tikepon* jacket
Civilized as we are.
We have learned not to learn from Darwin
To take a shower in the bathroom
To versify
Civilized as we are.
To build bridges
To make laws
To use condoms
Civilized as we are.
To play cards
To visit pagodas
To make nuclear warheads

Civilized as we are.
To learn to walk on the moon

To be vaccinated
To shut our doors
Civilized as we are.

[...]

6.

So...
Straight-faced
We've been predicting rain
With a knife and a fork
We've been relishing rabbit foetuses.
From our tiny telescope
We've been telescoping on a single star a million lights years away.
We've been fighting for the lift
To go down to the level of the four inferior existences.
Sipping wine, we've been listening to
The shells launched from Potemkin
We've been preserving
The Garden of Eden in formalin
We've been tailoring this-and-that-isms
To suit us.
Straight-faced
We've been declaring war
Ceasing hostilities
We've been felling trees
Planting trees
We've been getting married
Getting divorced.
Straight-faced
We've been role-playing
Not role-playing
We've been swimming downstream
Swimming upstream
We've been eating one half
Hawking up the other half.
Straight-faced
We've been fishing

Freeing fish.
Turning lies into truth
Truth into lies.
Fearing death
Not fearing death.

7.

The end of history
Prestige is money
Remain virtuous even when the whole world goes malicious
You can't wash in the same river twice
Feeling insecure, don't be impure
Save the Ozone
Everything stems from libido
War for peace
Who is Spartacus
l'existence précède l'essence.

8.

You…
For your living
For your happy living
Or
For your unhappy living
You need nothing
Even these sentences are redundant.

Translated by ko ko thett and James Byrne.

KHIN AUNG AYE was born 1956 in Rangoon and brought up in Rangoon, where he attended the university. He has published eleven collections of poetry, which include collaborations with leading poets and translators from Burma, among them Zeyar Lynn and his own cousin and early teacher Maw Rousseau. He is regarded as one of the great modern poets of Burmese poetry and his style emerged from close readings of the old masters in Burma, like Dagon Taya, and later in the 1980s, influenced by the workshops of Maung Tha Noe. In his early life as a poet in Burma Khin Aung Aye stuck to four-syllable verse, before becoming influenced by modernism (publishing significantly with leading modernist publisher Moe Way) and he now writes some of the most challenging, rewarding and intelligently-nuanced poetry written in the Burmese language. He lives in Bangkok and has recently read his work in England and South Korea.

gun and cheese

mickey mouse appears out of the red circle
the sketch of a ship drawn on blue tracing paper
towards invisible islands columbus hadn't discovered
the discovery of penicillin, its usefulness, and the never-ending
regrets of humans
the mysterious experiences of a kiss and its art of presentation
the unsmooth handing down to next generations
pounding gun-powder needs adjustment to get sparks all right
the way the cheese is moved without success

Translated by Maung Tha Noe.

Bones Will Crow: an anthology of Comtemporary Burmese Poetry, edited by ko ko thett and James Byrne, is forthcoming from Arc Publications in 2012.

REVIEWS

[...] marked forever
As her creature and her fool.

– Ruth Fainlight

About Suffering They Were Never Wrong

STEVEN MATTHEWS

Geoffrey Hill, *Clavics*, Enitharmon, £12, ISBN 978907587115;
Derek Mahon, *New Collected Poems*, Gallery Press, €20,
ISBN 978852355128

Both Geoffrey Hill and Derek Mahon are releasing a spate of work in the later part of their careers. Hill's *Clavics* is the second collection of a promised five to appear since mid-2007; Mahon's *New Collected* brings together work of fifty years, yet over a third of it comes from books published in the last six. What we find in each volume is a poet who is increasingly pushing something of his established style onto new grounds full of potential. Both late works take on new and urgent concerns, which directly confront their authors' established formal practices.

Strangely so, in the case of Hill's new book. *Clavics*, we are told, means "the science or alchemy of keys", and these thirty-two poems are shaped on the page so as to present, however approximately, some resemblance to a key. This is achieved in the manner of pattern poems: most well-known, perhaps, through George Herbert's 'The Altar' and 'Easter Wings'. Indeed, Hill's "keys" seem to be created by jamming a shape variant on the first upon the stanza shape of the second. Out of this visual punning Hill forms a twenty-line poem which balances upon an answering or variant ten lines. Typically, given the numerological interests that late Hill shares with late Yeats, in poem twenty Herbert's formal influence is confronted: "Herbert times and twists text hereby: / Balanced glass wit let-tipple into Grace."

Sitting on Hill's shoulder throughout is the shade of John Milton; as it has since the late style emerged in the mid-1990s. Hill's *Clavics* is an elegiac sequence for the Royalist musician William Lawes, killed in 1645 at the Battle of Chester. Milton had lauded Henry Lawes, William's brother and also a musician with Royalist sympathies, in a sonnet. Milton's praise for Henry centred upon his treatment of lyrics with "just note and accent", without wrenching the stress and intonation of the text in his setting. Hill's elaborate wringing of the language (he too "times and twists the text") to celebrate William Lawes contends that a Miltonic lyric smoothness is now often impossible to achieve. Typically for this late work, Hill deploys a variant of telegraphese, in which the "swarm- / Ing mass, the dense / Fluctuations of the material" are in danger of baffling the writer, to the extent that he proclaims that he will be "lucky" to drag much "Creative fire" from it.

If, here, "The grace of music is its dissonance / Unresolved beneath resolution", then an implication might be, as it was for T.S. Eliot, that the English Civil War was the moment at which the "material" of history and poetry, or poetry as history, became dense and fluctuating. Side-swiping at the recent financial crisis, as he does across the book, Hill suggests that, "at best", poetry might "Shake a crosspatched nation", but that it does so "At cost". Readers prepared to go with the inevitable vexations that the extremity of Hill's ambition here causes will experience the myriad passing bounties which *Clavics* conveys. What the book dramatizes through that ambition, more starkly than his other recent work, however, is the question as to *what* is eventually unlocked by this labour? "Alchemy" is a fool's game, even for international bankers to indulge, and there is much tom-fooling in the book. If, on the other hand, "clavics" is a "science", then its result in relation to Hill's demanding poetic experiment remains occluded, the "Creative fire" denied air.

Followers of Derek Mahon's career will breathe something of a collective sigh of relief upon opening his *New Collected Poems*. Aside from some silly tinkering around with poems' titles, this wilfully perverse custodian of his own output has left things relatively well alone since the last 'collected' edition of only twelve years ago. Rather than messing with the fabric of many of the poems (although the early tribute to MacNeice, here 'Carrowdore', now has a very different second stanza), Mahon has simply eliminated poems wholesale from the canon. Seemingly, one principle behind this has been to suppress the many, and it has to be said compelling, versions of classical and (largely) French texts, which have hitherto impelled and inflected his oeuvre. Some recent variants on Homer, though, oddly remain. On the other hand, several poems which have themselves become staples of critical work on the poet and his context now no longer appear. The early metamorphic wonder, 'The Apotheosis of Tins' has gone; the mid-career, amused meditation upon modernism, 'A Kensington Notebook' also. Interestingly, swathes of the recent books, such as (mercifully) the poems dubiously written for the fictitious Hindi poet Gopal Singh, from *An Autumn Wind* (2010), are not collected in the *New Collected*.

Like Hill, Mahon has increasingly seen poetic economy as in some sense performing a stricture upon the haphazard of finance and of narrow nationalisms. Although acknowledging the allure of 'Decadence' (the new title for the old book-length sequence *The Yellow Notebook*), the complex Byronic or Marvellian architecture of Mahon's stanzas has always offered its own countering stance:

> Magic survives only where blind profit,
> so quick on the uptake, takes no notice of it
> for ours is a crude culture dazed with money,
> a flighty future that would ditch its granny.

Although this is flippantly maintained, elsewhere and unexpectedly, such as in the Swiftian context of 'St. Patrick's Day', the mood can become plangent, as

> [...] we give ourselves to a vast corporate scheme
> where our true wit is devalued once again,
> our solitude known only to the rain.

Excoriating as Mahon's satire can be, the Baudelairean context of the solitary wanderer amongst others' fripperies remains.

Increasingly, though, it would seem that Mahon's former sense that poetry, at least, might transform the dross of the world has stalled before concern at the plight of 'Life on Earth' in this late, climate-change-blighted, time. In the late 1990s, "the bright garbage on the incoming wave" could still become, via Pasolini, subject to punning inquisition: "in the refuse of the world a new world is born". While Mahon shares with Hill a "rage" to see "material shaped" into poetry, he does so aware now that "The orchard withers but the birds sing on". Mahon's achievement has always been to adapt the seemingly stern discipline of his tight form to a conversational idiom that operates within a calm community of addressees and recipients (many poems are "*for*" friends and colleagues in the craft). Against the increasing threats to the planet, a capitalism astray, and continuing historical debilities, such geniality proffers its steady and wonderful appeal.

Steven Matthews's collection *Skying* appears from Waterloo Press in January.

Then Look Back

CHLOE STOPA-HUNT

Sean O'Brien, *November*, Picador, £8.99, ISBN 9780330535007

Sean O'Brien's new collection, *November*, opens by inviting its reader to "Look away just for a moment. / Then look back". This insistent, coaxing demand for reappraisal defines the book's engagement with literary tradition – lightly worn, but consummately understood – and directs our attention to its own "looking back", through the modes of elegy and memorial which it foregrounds. *November* is deeply rooted in O'Brien's earlier work: as far back as *The Frighteners* (1987), the reader was advised to "listen / For what I might mean when I stop", and this new collection offers a sustained, profoundly interrogative exploration of what O'Brien once called, in a short story, "the domain of Afterwards [...] where, secretly, you have always wished to be". Six previous collections have revealed a poet capable of accomplished modulations between wit, tenderness, and savagery, and this gift for synthesis allows O'Brien to orchestrate a genuinely novel and symphonic threnody from the fractious materials of bereavement and national decay.

'Fireweed', the concise lyric with which the collection begins, locates itself in "the silence / After the age of the train", but this silence is not only one of absence: it also forms the necessary condition for that "strong neglect" which is the poem's motive and subject in its lyrical capacity as a song of praise. The railway has long been a rich seam in O'Brien's poetics, and he uses it repeatedly and fluidly in *November* to figure loss. 'Narbonne' captures the whisk of sound from a passing train, and the subsequent stillness of streets "From which the sound has only now / Yet therefore utterly departed, which is why / I go on listening anyway". Fusing the fact of loss with the experience of it, these deceptively simple lines (the anti-intuitive distribution of line-breaks is much more artful than it appears) echo earlier poems from the memorial core of the collection – particularly 'Elegy', 'The Lost Book', and 'Novembrists', all of which repay multiple readings. 'Elegy', O'Brien's poem for his mother, belies its straightforward title by gesturing towards the impossibilities (even the importunities) of the elegiac endeavour:

> This elegy's a metaphysical excuse,
> A sick-note meant to keep you back
> A little longer, though you have no need to hear
> What I must say, because your life was yours,
> Mysterious and prized, a yard, a universe away.

These lines testify to the ontological interests of O'Brien's elegies, which never simply lament but concern themselves with being, unbeing, and the slow processes of vanishing: "the task of reversion, this sweet degradation", he calls it in one of the collection's fine landscape-elegies, 'Railway Lands', a poem which recalls the end of *The Dry Salvages*, and the Larkin of *High Windows*.

The end of 'Elegy' revisits O'Brien's fascination with stand-ins and doubles, which in *November* takes on a pervasively wistful note. In the Dantesque milieu of 'On the Toon', the poet's nymph-like guide is subsumed into a parade of interchangeable losses: "her face appeared on posters everywhere, / As missing child and teenage runaway, one face / For all those we have carelessly mislaid". In this phantasmagoric mode, the poet can be reassured that "Her disappearance / Was a test", but the other disappearances enshrined by *November* prove less playful, more determinate, though they too are tests of a sort: tests of love, tests of elegy. Several poems in the second half of the book address fellow poets: 'Michael', 'The Landing-Stage', 'Dinner at Archie's', 'Porteriana', and 'Leavetaking' all appear to hint, through stylistic echoes and occasional moments of graceful ventriloquism, at a resurrective poetics which might summon O'Brien's friends and influences back onto the page. Yet they ultimately bow to the mannerly demands crystallised in an image from 'Leavetaking', one of the poems for Peter Porter, in which O'Brien conjures "these so-courteous deaths, who sweep / Their maidens up and down the shore / In perfect silence on their light fantastic feet".

O'Brien's poems show an urgency of invention, which – coupled with his usual command of metre and pacing – lifts them far above any threat of elegiac torpor. In 'Bruges-la-Morte', sparking couplets revivify the European decay chronicled in Georges Rodenbach's 1892 novel of the same name, oscillating between registers from the biblical, to the medical, to the idiomatic: "all flesh is adipose", the poem insists. This damaged, decadent Europe complements the collection's interest in a waning England, and proves an engaging setting for poems such as 'Jeudi Prochain', in which O'Brien gives us a portrait of the Muse as a sometime Fascist collaborator and mercurial provocateuse, "Who in one instant shyly bleeds a pig / Beside a sunlit window in Provence / And next is all severity in furs". The striking, unexplained exactitude of "shyly" exemplifies the poetic assurance of *November*, which offers many such moments of achieved lyricism. These are pre-eminently thoughtful poems – their literary underpinnings stretching from Marlowe to Rimbaud to Auden – but it is O'Brien's lyric gift which succeeds again and again in making from this great richness, great simplicities.

Chloe Stopa-Hunt is a poet and critic from Hampshire.

Through The Open Door

ADAM THORPE

Jaan Kaplinski, *Selected Poems*, Bloodaxe, £12, ISBN 9781852248895;
Michael Longley, *A Hundred Doors*, Cape, £10, ISBN 9780224091381

Estonia and Ireland have various things in common: the haunting beauty of bogs and boulders beyond the farmland; a tragic history of occupation, violence and exile; a profound sense of homeland; and an awareness of being on the margins (latterly of two empires) yet central to trade – and with an unfortunate strategic importance in the case of Estonia.

All this is relevant to Jaan Kaplinski and Michael Longley, and might go some way to explaining why they seem poetic cousins. Their chief interest is nature, or what Richard Jefferies called "the anti- or ultra-human, and [which] has no concern with man" (*The Story of My Heart*, 1883). They are romantics, in the loose sense of being primarily concerned with their own individual relationship with nature, a relationship which even in exultation will always fall short of the full embodiment they crave. If Kaplinski believes that "every single thing / contains all other things", he makes it clear that this is more repeated mantra than concrete reality; the closest this awareness comes to being realised in poetry is in flashes of inspired metaphor. Mystic oneness would be inexpressible, mere silence.

The poet-persona is always in the act of failing to cross the border between consciousness and the other: that very "border" or "wall", as Kaplinski describes it, being built mainly of language. Both poets are like ecological troubadours in love with what is unattainable. As Kaplinski puts it:

> Running for milk I saw wood sorrel in bloom
> to the left of the path, and my mind became restless,
> feeling its helplessness [...]

This separation is inevitable, and for the poetry to have force actually desirable. Kaplinski's work has a great deal of force. For this reviewer, at least, it triggered an affection for Estonia – back in the 1980s – which has only been strengthened by repeated visits to the country itself. The poems evoke a very particular sense of place; perhaps it is relevant that Estonia is the oldest homeland in Europe, in terms of identifiable borders and an indigenous people, and that it contains some of the last remaining patches of the continent's primaeval forest.

If Kaplinski's work is imbued with Buddhist teachings, Longley (born in Belfast) is more ecumenical: while *A Hundred Doors* refers to the Byzantine church on Paros (Our Lady of the Hundred Doors), he calls himself "a sentimental atheist". This is typically modest and self-denigrating; Kaplinski is more given to a kind of contemplative grandeur buttressed (rather than undercut) by physical detail:

> God has left us: I felt this clearly
> loosening the earth around a rhubarb plant.
> It was black and moist. I don't know where he is,
> only a shelf full of sacred books remains of him [...]

God's absence leaves the poet free as well as "fearful". Like the music of his compatriot Arvo Pärt, Kaplinski's poetry is threaded with silence. Silence often appears juxtaposed with the ticking of time, and stands for both death and a wordless, supra-natural 'reality' already present in Kaplinski's first translated collection, *The Same Sea in Us All* (1985): its title referred to both Buddhist consolation and a shared national suffering. The poet was born in 1941, lost his father to a labour camp, and referred to his childhood as "a time of repression, fear and poverty". Silence, then, was something imposed as well as treasured, and even now Estonians show a certain care or caution with words. Life is a serious business, and happiness is fragile – the poet's fear is that "some of the pieces of the mosaic will disappear: the nightingales will not come, the dung-beetle will not fly". National vulnerability is also ecological.

Aside from shifts in form (from lines of one word to prose poetry),

Kaplinski's poems have generally kept to a familiar structure; they begin with an action ("I got out of a bus"), continue through metaphysical crisis triggered mysteriously by that action ("I jumped into silence / and there was no ground to step on"), and close in tentative consolation through an interweaving of the present's immediacy ("White birch trunks. The Big Boulder") with personal memories; a return, in other words, to the inner self, but one which is suspended in time and space. Kaplinski likens memories to vanished snow-tracks in Estonia's sudden spring; they are there and not there. Time, death and suffering preside, but, as he wittily concludes in a poem beginning "Death will not come from outside", "death will not outlive us". This is an excellent and welcome *Selected*, and includes some impeccable work "written in English".

Michael Longley's continuing response (at least in his later collections) to humanity's fall from natural grace is to name, lovingly, the various particulars of nature, from oystercatcher to marram grass, found not only in his cherished "soul-arena" of Carrigskeewaun in County Mayo but also in Italy, the Shetlands, Greece and elsewhere.

The first word in *A Hundred Doors* is "alone" ('Call'). The narrator worries about a friend's solitude in the Carrigskeewaun cottage: a serious concern for a poet whose collections are imbued with a sense of hospitable gatherings, of friendship and of family love:

> Is it too late to phone him? Is it midnight yet?
> That could be me, a meadow pipit calling out.

Is the pipit actually the ring of the phone? How can the poet-speaker hear the pipit, anyway? How would he know that there are "three dolphins passing the Carricknashinnagh shoal?" The poem, thus ambiguously announcing both presence and absence, ends on a grim note: "How snugly the meadow pipit fits the merlin's foot." This, something neither the "friend" nor the poet can see, seems to have a metaphorical energy, the "snugly" vying with the violent death of the bird who stands in for the (phone) call of friendship. There is a sub-text here that we are not quite privy to, but which is the more effective for being unstated.

This is the Longley way – his genius, even. A brief meditation on his "final resting place", a promontory now visible through the new window of the title, ends on "a blur of bog-cotton, afterfeathers from a thousand preenings." The image is of a bird's discarded plumage, but also possibly of the "preenings" of poems. Another poet might have made the possible certain. Longley lets in the silence. This delicacy of touch cancels any potential mawkishness in the volme's multiple celebrations of grandchildren ("I carry you into the house [...] Conor Michael, grandson number four"), or of married love, or in the finely-turned elegies for friends and neighbours. Longley's grief for the sufferings on the Western Front (his father was decorated for gallantry: "I shiver behind him on the fire-step") is extended here.

Both poets treasure the child's-eye view of creation, of the smaller and more secret doors. One of the charms of Longley's new volume is that even the slighter poems share fully in its rich "language of flowers", its "Sea-roar-surrounded [...] quietude". The many questions posed remain unanswered: but that – as Kaplinski puts it in a poem pre-dating our use of the doubt-free Web – is because poetry

is a particular sort of ignorance. And that
is much harder to learn than knowing.

Adam Thorpe's new collection, *Voluntary*, will be published by Jonathan Cape in March 2012.

Sibyl

KIM MOORE

Ruth Fainlight, *New and Collected Poems*, Bloodaxe, £20,
ISBN 9781852248857

This very substantial *New and Collected Poems* includes work spanning a period of fifty years, and draws from over a dozen collections and chapbooks.

Sometimes, collections of work by distinguished poets can seem like an album of 'Greatest Hits'. However this volume has clearly been put together with care. The new poems at the opening set out for the first time reader Ruth Fainlight's main concerns: ageing, the moon, careful observation of the natural world and engagement with myths and fables. As the reader moves on to her first collection, *Cages*, published in 1966, it becomes apparent that these themes were present right from the beginning, and so begins a slow unwrapping and exploration throughout the various collections, allowing 'new' and 'old' poems to speak and answer one another.

Fainlight's moon has differing meanings and connotations. In 'Borrowed Time', it is appealed to as an entity being able to give life or extend it. In 'Dawn Blue', the moon is likened to a woman's face. Later on, 'Another Full Moon', the title poem of Fainlight's fourth, 1976, collection, is portrayed as torturer:

> [...] for all my days I shall bear
> The scars of her torture, marked forever
> As her creature and her fool.

The first poem included from that collection, 'Vertical' sees her challenging the labels attached to her, writing that speech "sets me free / From whomsoever's definition: Jew. Woman. Poet". It seems incongruous that, in 2011, this conversation about labelling poets must still go on.

Fainlight returns to the subject of the Muse, often considered the preserve of male writers, throughout her work. Muse poems are dotted throughout the book, but in *Sibyls and Others* she explores these marginal female figures with the gift of prophecy. This whole set of poems is compelling – but none more so than the last, 'Introspection of a Sibyl'. It's tempting to replace "Sibyl" with "poet" throughout:

> If only I could be aware of what is happening
> in that void, that gap, that murky, fathomless cleft
> where space and time must exist
> between inspiration and the sound of my own voice;
> the truth I never once have heard
> a moment earlier than my listeners.

The poems about the process of ageing are also extraordinary. In 'A Different Form', Fainlight compares fruit going rotten to the "age-blotched arms of a gaunt old man"; but then she goes further and says that what consumes food (and flesh) has

> the same immortal
> energy as the one about to be born,

that matter can change but never die,
that nothing is wasted – although
each time it takes a different form.

'Facts About Ants' and 'The Lace Wing' view the natural environment with a painter's eye. In Fainlight's world, however, nothing is quite what it seems. 'Pigeons at Villa Belmonte' tells us that:

> [...] pigeons caged and left
> Will pluck each other bare and bleeding,
> That they're more murderous
> Than wolves, with no inborn restraint.

It is this imaginative understanding of the commonplace which continually engages and entertains the reader in this substantial collection from one of Britain's most distinguished poets.

The year, Kim Moore has received both an Eric Gregory Award and *Poetry Review*'s Geoffrey Dearmer Prize.

Unsentimental Idylls

LAVINIA SINGER

Bernard O'Donoghue, *Farmers Cross*, Faber, £9.99, ISBN 9780571268603;
Mary Oliver, *Swan*, Bloodaxe, £9.95, ISBN 9781852249076

Collective terms can be misleading. Mary Oliver and Bernard O'Donoghue are labelled 'nature poets', yet remain worlds apart in how they engage with their surroundings. The American's "literature of praise" is far from Irish poet Bernard O'Donoghue's meditations, which are altogether more probing and sombre.

Named after a region in County Cork, *Farmers Cross* continues O'Donoghue's by now familiar exploration of landscape and place in *Outliving* (2003) and *Here nor There* (1999). He is interested not only in what the eye can observe, but in what has been witnessed and absorbed. The book's epigraph, from haiku poet Matsuo Bashō, is telling: "Of all the many places mentioned in poetry, / the exact location of most is not known for certain." Here, the "exact" and "certain" are transformed over time, as personal memory, public history and literary tradition take their toll. The collection is rooted in domestic routine and rurality, and uses the cycle of seasons, farmyard motifs, place names and colourful dialect. Excerpts from Dante and *Piers Plowman* sit amidst the poet's own countryside observations; from Lady's Smock flowers with their "mauve elegance", to a humming kingfisher and that "rarer glimpse" – the otter ('Hover'). Distinctive characters such as Jer Mac, "the greatest breaker of horses" and Jack Sweeney, "injured at Verdun", are made familiar.

However, these are no sentimental idylls. Amidst the larger-than-life figures from childhood lurk the ghosts of those whose names sit above the poems, in dedications that mirror tombstone epitaphs. Ancient ring-forts and prehistoric stone have been bulldozed in 'City Planning', risking oblivion if not for their unearthing by aerial photography. American tourists in 'The Old Graveyard' "spray shaving-foam" on graves to decipher faded inscriptions. *Farmers Cross* is about rediscovering what is hidden beneath the surface: the ancient world that shores up our modern one like an imperceptible skeleton.

Unsurprisingly for a scholar of Old English, O'Donoghue's lyrics ache with the weight of the ancient world. Included is an exquisite translation of the Anglo Saxon elegy 'The Wanderer'. Exiled retainer becomes "refugee", whilst casual-sounding translations – "something / to turn my hand to" – reflect the poet's penchant for colloquialism. The archaic format of gnomic phrasing and *ubi sunt* topos are updated to a contemporary world of radio, machines and bombs, highlighting the Anglo-Saxon poem's continued relevance for modern-day wanderers: whether the 'Bona-Fide Travellers' of the opening poem, or O'Donoghue's own "wanderings across the seas" when he migrated to England after his father's death. Immigration, the Iraq war, concentration camps… O'Donoghue does not shy from the explicitly political. 'Man of my Time' is 'after' Quasimodo, the Italian poet whose own writing was profoundly affected by his experience of the Second World War. Here the agelessness of war, its hand-me-down inevitability inherited from our forefathers, is articulated in a jaded voice:

> You've seen it all – the burnt jeeps by Basra,
> the gallows, the rack, the wheel of torture.

The chiastic pattern of iambs and anapaests create their own fatalistic rhythm. Violence and destruction remain something as determined as the succession of seasons and passing of time.

Swan is Mary Oliver's twentieth volume, written in her seventy-fourth year after a writing career spanning more than five decades. Appropriate, therefore, to begin by asking: "What can I say that I have not said before?" Her answer is "to say it again", revisiting beloved themes of nature, solitude and beauty and communicating them with renewed intensity and vigour.

Unlike the sense of separation and distance that eerily floods O'Donoghue's poetic landscape, Oliver is firmly 'at one' with her surroundings. This poet heads to the fields to "lay down / among the weeds and the grasses" ('How Many Days'). Her solitude is by volition and rarely extends to loneliness, whether on the beach at dawn or under the leafy heights of trees. In 'How I Go to the Woods', she revels in a Wordsworthian "bliss of solitude". The use of first-person, simple cadence and matter-of-fact present tense in this prose-poem are preferred techniques throughout the book, and reflect the comforting routine of her excursions, unravelling with a storyteller's ease.

This poetry combines the Romantic tradition of the West with characteristics of the East: Sufi ecstasy, Buddhist mindfulness and spirituality. In 'Of Time', she alludes directly to Rumi, Li Po, and the Iranian mystic Hafiz. Several lyrics conjure a world of dancing and singing, whilst others play with the haiku format, written as nuggets of pure feeling and elation. A meditation on "all the imponderables" of life, in 'Trying to Be Thoughtful in the First Brights of Dawn', is interrupted by a caesural rush of emotion:

> [...] But, but –
> excuse me now, please; it's morning, heavenly bright,
> and my irrepressible heart begs me to hurry on
> into the next exquisite moment.

This "exquisite passion" and "flame-like" ecstasy that explodes and enjambs on the page is what Walter Pater so exuberantly expounds in his Conclusion to *The Renaissance*, an experience comparable to Joyce's 'epiphany' or a Woolfian 'moment of being'. In Oliver's philosophy, emotion is superior to reason. Nature is elevated to teacher, as in 'The Poet Dreams of the Classroom", where the poetic persona yearns for a knowledge found out of doors, defying her teacher's monosyllabic, authoritarian commands: "Sit down, he said".

Despite this resistance to instruction and command, it is Oliver's own preacher-like tone that can mar the purity of her expression. Urgent pleas that we share her vision cause opposite effects, such as the persistent needling in the title-poem 'Swan':

> And did you feel it, in your heart, how it pertained to everything?
> And have you too finally figured out what beauty is for?
> And have you changed your life?

Rather than leaving us with the exquisite vision of the swan "rising into the silvery air, / an armful of white blossoms" to form our own conclusions, (a technique used by Imagist poets of the early twentieth century, also influenced by the art of the haiku) Oliver is keen to provide a homily to condition our response. More evidence from 'More Evidence I': "With what words can I convince you of the / casualness with which the white swans fly?"

Her drive throughout this collection for us "not to miss anything" – encouraging close observation of the world around us – is an eagle-eyed scrutiny that O'Donoghue shares, as indeed do all fine poets.

Lavinia Singer won the 2010 Newdigate Prize.

Our Singing Language

DAVID MORLEY

Ilija Jovanović, *News from the Other World: Poems in Romani*,
Francis Boutle Publishers, £9.99, ISBN 9781903427545;
Claire Crowther, *Incense*, Flarestack Poets, £4.50, ISBN 9781906480271;
Brendan Kennelly, *The Essential Brendan Kennelly: Selected Poems*,
eds. Terence Brown and Michael Longley, with CD, Bloodaxe,
£12, ISBN 9781852249045

There is no pure Romani language: there are several living, vivid, ricocheting dialects. These dialects sometimes take a loan from other tongues: language is absorbed as it is travelled through. The porosity of Romani dialects can seem to resemble the porosity of English, except for one distinction. English, for all its riches, is a language of colonisation and globalisation; Romani, for its treasures, is a language of the invisible or enslaved. The Gurbet Romani dialect, for example, is influenced linguistically by centuries of enslavement of the Roma in Romania (the group term *Gurbet* means *foreign work* or *aliens*).

The Gurbet Roma group, like the Kalderaš and Lovara, is known for independence and entrepreneurship. A number of writers have arisen from it, the most prominent being Ilija Jovanović, whose first collection of poems *Bündel/Bod o* was published in Romani (and German translation) in the year 2000. *News from the Other World: Poems in Romani* is a bilingual selected poems. It opens with the writer's memories of childhood – accounts of the casual, unconscious racism of non-gypsy "friends" – as well as a short history of Roma people. The body of the book is made up of poems about settlements, hazards of travel, identity, love, childhood and salvation. These make for strong if, at times, severe reading: dark notes abound, *duende* is evoked and Jovanović's Romani diction has fine, wry attack. Romani is phonetic, so you can listen in to his voice through reading the poems as you find them. To get the flavour of this poet, try sounding the buzz-note consonants and dammed-up internal rhymes at the close of 'Lost World':

> Traden amen pe sa o them.
> Amen d as thaj d as
> ni d anas kaj thaj d i kaj.

(They chase us across the whole world.
We move on and on, having no idea
when this will end, or where to go.)

Jovanović calls Romani "our singing language", and like English it certainly possesses qualities that pass beyond meaning: the sound of sense, the sound of sensuality, and the sound of a group's shared sensibility. The poems collected here are capably translated by Melitta Depner. My sole criticism is that the concentration and energy of Jovanović's dialect sometimes carry abstractedly or blandly into English. The poet's attack and dark palette are what vanish in translation. To take a fairly typical example, from 'I Have No Home', the syntactical crackle, alliterative strut and resignation registered by the line-break of "Corope, bokh, maripe, mundǎriṗe / traden ma than thaneste te d av" registers in translation as dejected prose: "Poverty, hunger and violence / drive me from place to place". The Roma are indeed a victimised people, but do not wish to behave or sound like victims – or be ventriloquised into that role. What I am saying is that the poems work best in Romani, but you do not need to be a Romani speaker, nor a specialist in the Gurbet dialect, to get something out of this attractive and truthful book of poems. It is probably a tiny miracle it has been allowed to exist and it is a welcome addition to Romani writing in English translation.

Claire Crowther spent several years as an editor and journalist in the weight management industry. The subject of her pamphlet-length sequence *Incense* is body fat, a subject "relevant to many readers but rarely written about" sayeth The Blurb of Truth. Crowther's chosen poetic form is the, as she says "aptly named", *fatras*. The fatras arose in the fourteenth century France from the body of another form, the *fatrasie*, "a type of verse that exploits the unreasonable, the ridiculous and the grotesque" according to Lambert Porter's essay *La Fatrasie et le Fatras* (1960). The subjects of these old poems were surreal five centuries before Surrealism: a cheese sneezes, an onion brays, a basin chants a vigil, a flying castle sews an oven. Such medieval play demanded medieval rigour. In the *fatras*, two lines, evocative and courtly in tenor, launched the following eleven lines, furnishing the first and last lines and giving the poem its phrasal momentum and framing. Rule one for the *fatras* was to begin sharply and finish shapely; rule two insisted that reality is dreamlike. Hence this new example of the form from Claire Crowther:

Ask a woman who's lost four stone
from side to side like a throat cut.

Ask a women who's lost four stone
of (mostly) fat:
what is the difference?
Capacity to jump and run?

'Sure. But – as if snow melted
exposing tracks in tarmac
and the weediness of old
grass, this soaked ground –
my age has been uncovered.
Drawn mouth, a neck scored
from side to side like a throat cut.'   ('Untitled')

This conflation of fat and *fatras* could, at first glance, appear whimsical, even too insistently willed. My view is that the entire sequence is a minor revelation - an almost outrageously blessed ravelling of traditional form and contemporary subject. The subject is treated with truth and respect, yet the old form is given fresh tone and turn. Although Crowther follows the form's strictures to the letter, she is shrewd too, carving her own patterns. 'Let Us Now Praise Adipose Tissue' recreates the shape of "Two long chains / of fatty acids linked / by a glycerol backbone". This poem also demonstrates deeper strengths in the language chosen: Crowther uses scientific terminology to cunning poetic purpose, and she also uses that precise language accurately. Like Marianne Moore, she is able to locate the poetry asleep in the language of science, even dare I say in the language of weight management.

Brendan Kennelly is certainly an essential poet but his editors, Michael Longley and Terence Brown, have done him a favour by distilling his burgeoning oeuvre to the one hundred and ten poems in this volume, and the thirty-six poems on the accompanying CD (Kennelly is a highly skilled spoken word artist). This is a strong introduction to the work, and the editors are refreshingly candid about the poet's lyric and epic strengths as well – as his occasional failures of rigour (there are worse crimes than over-writing or writing too much). What comes across in *The Essential Brendan Kennelly* is the poet's spiritual generosity, a tonic sense of wonder and a project that allows new readers to reach the core of Kennelly's poetry without being tripped up by thirty slim and not-so-slim volumes.

David Morley's most recent collection is *Enchantment* (Carcanet, 2010). He is Professor of Writing at Warwick University.

Gestalt With Smart Cars

TIM LIARDET

Re:, Ahren Warner, Donut Press, £5.00, ISBN 9780644541;
Six Children, Mark Ford, Faber £9.99, ISBN 9780571273324;
Terrific Melancholy, Roddy Lumsden, Bloodaxe, £8.95, ISBN 9781852249083;
Changeling, Clare Pollard, Bloodaxe, £8.95, ISBN 9781852249113

Ahren Warner is a real discovery. His poems bear the unmistakable gift of concision. Behind them moves the presence of a high intelligence and every page of his debut collection bursts with some matter to expiate. Not only do the poems have a good sound but they are lyrically original; unlike many contemporary poets Warner has made his peace with the first person singular. It takes the merest glance to get quite how unusually evolved his irony is, especially if you happened to start with 'About suffering they were never wrong, The Old Masters':

> Though, when it comes to breasts, it's a different story.
> Cranach, for example, never seems to have progressed
> beyond his pubescent attempts at apprenticeship:
>
> tennis balls sewn to a pillow of hay, fingers coming
> to terms with the concept of foreplay. So too
> with Titian, whose Venus bares handleless plungers
>
> or the fruits of a template mocked up at Bellini's [...]

Such suavity, such precocious wit, is repeated throughout the twenty-four short pages of this excellent little book. Already Warner's poetics include experimentation – at this stage largely the mysteries of the step-line and Burnside-like fragmentations – but there's no naive attempt falsely to ghettoise this from the less experimental. This is where the *gestalt* lives, in integrated strains of artistic exploration. The strains yield fully achieved poems, and what is more they *collect*. There is no doubt in my mind *Re:* is a collection, and a very accomplished one. Individually, the poems are so lean-burn they zig-zag as nippily as Smart Cars through the diesel-guzzling gridlock that currently is UK poetry.

Mark Ford's *Six Children* is full of similarly nippy individual poems that might well have been written specifically for high profile competitions and might equally well have won each of them. They are blessed with peculiar energy and lightness of touch. They have a very particular way of stylising their own excitement. The puzzlement of the collection, however, is the manner in which these poems explode away from a centre that is not quite there. One looks in vain for a centre of gravity and finds only more poems. Unlike Warner, Ford uses the slipperiest species of first person singular. And his objects of affection are wide-ranging, taking in Hart Crane, Catullus, Pliny the Elder, Bashō, to name but a few. His talent for imagistic brio is one of his principal hallmarks:

> One inch
> of Emotion, One inch
> of Ash, I read, in fiery letters, on a skin-
> tight T-shirt
> passing, a little too close, at rush-hour, under the soaring stanchions
> of Hungerford Bridge [...]   ('Masse und Macht')

The absence of a centre, though, that is to say the place where his poetics might be anchored by *weltanschauung* or ideology, made it difficult for me to find a trajectory through the book. There's no doubting the high air-fuel ratio of *Six Children*; the poems certainly have plenty of nip. But I found myself whispering that word again: *gestalt*?

The title poem of Roddy Lumsden's *Terrific Melancholy*, extending over twelve pages, is about an unsuccessful love affair. It would have been more effective if its thirty six stanzas, of ten lines each, had been halved. As love poems go, it's the strangest I've read. This is largely due to the lack of sensuous diction. The poem defies all conventions of address by reading like an annual report from the Research Centre for Catchment Hydrology:

> and we do not play a scene together
> and we will not make a scene together [...]

This couplet, a plot-driver for the more than-three hundred line poem, is inauspicious. Most noticeable in the pages which follow is how little attention the love-object gets compared with the ample coverage afforded the love-victim. The victim is always present, sometimes a tad too hairily: "I am / an ape reaching through bars." Like victims do, he runs himself a bath, rueing his luck: "It's love I want, and the song which / follows love." This poem, like the book, is the sum of its parts.

The last section of the book, on the other hand, is comprised of 'American poems'. Lumsden's titles read like ersatz Americana: 'Chinatown Funeral Motorcade', 'Freight Train Interlude', 'Holiday Melisma Overdub', 'Highway Forgiving Song', 'Hallowe'en Downpour Downer' and so forth. Such 'tourist' poems merely have the effect of misappropriating American mythology while simultaneously throwing into sharper relief their essentially parochial provenance. Elsewhere, in 'Daredevil', the Lumsden king-making instinct seeps through its own facades in a poem which is either about the Scottish Crossbill dressed as Roddy Lumsden or Roddy Lumsden dressed as the Scottish Crossbill: "I wish to be / the captain of the things that have no name."

Though her title clashes with a Clint Eastwood movie, which'll probably upset her more than it does Clint Eastwood, Clare Pollard's *Changeling* is altogether different. Her collection of forty-three poems is well managed and has a good deal of charm. It is a book driven by narrative purpose, and the relaxed but by no means loose line moves with a very brisk tempo. What's more she can turn a mean sonnet, when required, as in 'First sunflowers':

> I watch them as they lean against the wall,
> like lads behind a bike-shed for a smoke.
> They nod, all skinny legs and awkward-tall;
> the leaves shrug in the breeze. Their faces glow.

And there is a sense in this collection of a book which is more than the sum of its parts. One of the reasons for this is that Pollard has understood the extent to which atmosphere is revelation. Again and again she conjures the physical aura within which something is to be said, within which something is to be expiated, as in 'Whitby': "Whirlpools of gulls whip over harbour – / clouds of yellow eyes – / and the stone sea's fearsome, melted /and roused to terrible passion." She can also put a good satirical spin on things, when required, thereby adding a sort of psychological dimension to the entire collection, as in 'Revelations': "God spoke to me /and he said tell my children to avoid prawns or condoms, / behead homosexuals, whip women who like trousers, / and 'I love Utah.'"

Tim Liardet's *The Storm House* (Carcanet) was published in July.

After The Objectivists

DAI GEORGE

Sara Berkeley, *The View from Here*, Gallery, E11.95, ISBN 9781852354978;
Martyn Crucefix, *Hurt*, Enitharmon, £9.99, ISBN 9781904634973;
Dennis Nurkse, *Voices Over Water*, CB Editions, £7.99, ISBN 9780956107367;
Anthony Rudolf, *Zigzag*, Carcanet, £9.95, ISBN 9781847771100;
John Siddique, *Full Blood*, Salt, £9.99, ISBN 9781844718245

I once saw Dennis Nurkse talk on George Oppen, the great American Objectivist poet and left-wing activist. One line from that evening still sticks in the mind. According to Nurkse, Oppen found it difficult to use enjambment: not out of any limitation in his craft, but as a result of his own Olympian aesthetic and ethical standards. "Every line break *cost* Oppen," Nurkse said, eyebrow furrowed. That's as perceptive, gnomic and elusive a critical insight as you're likely to find. What I think it boils down to is this: Oppen thought poetry should be more than a euphonic, sensitive arrangement of language; that it has the power to interrogate, denature and rally against the language of capitalism and oppression (for Oppen, rather the same thing). Hence, we should beware of the musical component of poetry and – in particular – the line, the formal device that most renders a poem musical. We should look before we leap down the page.

Regardless of whether Nurkse was right about Oppen, his words stand as a great example of someone creating the taste by which he would be appreciated. *Voices Over Water*, an old collection being reissued by the estimable CB Editions, confirms Nurkse as an heir to Oppen's moral seriousness and artistry. A book-length narrative sequence, it tells – elliptically – the story of a married couple's forced emigration from Estonia to Canada in the early twentieth century. This may sound like a recipe for dour, right-on gruel, but the results in Nurkse's hands are anything but. The collection comprises delicate, dreamlike lyrics, shifting between two epic, wintry landscapes. In 'Snowbound', the husband describes life during a sickly, housebound winter in the new world of Canada: "December climbs to the top of the sash, / the sky thickens and darkens like kneaded batter." Disoriented in a landscape that seems at once familiar and alien, he mourns how

[...] that will to erase all obstacles,
that once crippled me, has grown bland
in this house whose doors
buckle in a wind I cannot feel.

These are not poems to puzzle through. They are approachable in a way that much poetry isn't, committed to providing lucid testimony. However, they unmistakably share with Oppen a belief in the significance of the line. In 'Factions' we see this very clearly. It describes the visits from thugs ("not men / given to subtleties", in Nurkse's deadpan phrasing) and the narrator's attempt to give an account of "which side [he] was on" that won't lead to immediate arrest:

At first I said: God:
meaning, nothing: but later
even that was not a safe answer…
I explained that I was on the side
of God's poverty but not my own
and against the divinity of the poor
except in my case [...]

Each line break enacts a twist in the encounter: a sarcastic, internal clarification ("God: / meaning, nothing"); a glimpse toward the future ("later / even that was not a safe answer"); a hasty modification for the benefit of the authorities ("against the divinity of the poor / except in my case"). This is how speech and thought work in a culture where what you say can have consequences for your life.

To go from work such as Nurkse's, which patrols each line break as though it were a border crossing, to John Siddique's *Full Blood* is at first a shock. Siddique is an expansive, public poet, and his forms create the space for oration: lines feel like approximate markers for breath rather than fixed boundaries. Siddique's fulsomeness can lead him astray, into baggy forms and woolly spirituality; yet it's this very quality that allows him to ramble into moments of excellence. 'Love Poem' is a fragment about a woman trying to make ends meet by working multiple jobs, who as a result fails "to notice the sleeping animal of her body, / how it cannot wake up to open its claws". This image hinges on a brilliant, counterintuitive observation: that deep sleep is something that needs time to come alive, not a brief period of nullity.

Whereas effusion can be the making or undoing of Siddique's poetry, in

Sara Berkeley's *The View from Here* it is more of a general setting; evidence of a friendly attitude towards the world. The fourth line in the book reads, "O thirsty water, O hungry food," in apparent sincerity. It makes you wonder whether Berkeley is either wilfully or blithely disinterested in contemporary poetry's postures of irony and self-reproach – and is actually quite refreshing. Later, in 'Oak', she declares, "I came to you for love and comfort and shelter", and you can imagine many readers finding similar sanctuary in this well crafted, good-natured, if sentimental collection.

No such comforts will be found in *Zigzag*, a bracing hotchpotch of a book that sees Anthony Rudolf return to poetry after a long spell concentrating on criticism, memoir and translations. There are few greater turn-offs than a poet who gives you the impression that he would struggle to string a sentence together in prose. Rudolf is the opposite: learned, rigorous, the type of poet who back-ends his collection with paragraphs of illuminating notes on the context behind each part (there are five in all across *Zigzag*, each with a very defined remit and occasion). Most interesting is the section titled 'Joseph Rudolf, my Zeida'. This formally audacious sequence takes the shape of a fragmented interview transcript between the author and his grandfather (originally taped in 1975, the note tells us, when Joseph was ninety-two).

The parallels with Nurkse are striking. Both *Voices Over Water* and 'Joseph Rudolf...' bear eloquent testament to a particular time of stress, dispersal and persecution in European Jewish history. Both tell their story – in very different ways – through the lens of an individual emigration. It may or may not be a coincidence that, in his notes, Rudolf pays tribute to Charles Reznikoff for pioneering the poem-as-transcript technique: Reznikoff was an associate of Oppen and a fellow Objectivist. What Nurkse and Rudolf don't share, however, is a tonal or formal strategy, and it's here that we see Nurkse's departure from his Objectivist forebears is stronger than his debts. Ultimately Nurkse isn't opposed to music; his is very careful and glacial, but beautiful and lyric all the same. Rudolf, on the other hand, revolts directly against poetry's sonic conventions: 'Joseph Rudolf...' is filled with rude editorial interjections along the lines of, "(This describes what happened when he wrote his only poem [section 18 above]. Sure enough, he stopped writing poems)". This creates its own strange dissonances.

For a poet of lyrical gifts comparable to Nurkse's, we could do worse than look to Martyn Crucefix and his fine collection *Harm*. He too tends towards short, gaunt lines, demonstrating that this austere music needn't work only in support of big historical themes (although, with a seven-part

poem on war called 'More Than It Comes To', he's not averse to them either).
'Calling in the Dark' is a moving pre-elegy for the speaker's aging parents.
Meeting them in a city pub, he looks out of the window to observe how

> Even London translates
> into something beautiful
> as buses idle at the lights
> quivering with spring rain.

Here short lines create a tentative aesthetic epiphany in the midst of the
mundane, the urban and rainy. Moving to the next line, though, we
understand why the mood is hesitant:

> Yet for the eldest two
> the hours and minutes run:
> the journey home is long,
> both liable to fall [...]

With an exquisite little shift, the same length of line comes to embody the
faltering confidence of the elderly. And because his parents have lost self-
belief, so has the speaker; what once would have been a pleasant outing has
degraded into a fraught ritual, endured rather than enjoyed. The cost of this
transformation is etched into every sad, precisely monitored line break.

Dai George is a poet and critic working towards his first collection, due from Seren in 2013.

Of Art And Vanity

TARA BERGIN

Gwyneth Lewis, *Sparrow Tree*, Bloodaxe, £8.95, ISBN 9781852248994;
Carole Satyamurti, *Countdown*, Bloodaxe, £8.95, ISBN 9781852249120

> and the dress is both work of art and a vanity
> and the vanity is a 'yes!' you give yourself
> though your self dissolves in a badinage of birdsong
> — Carole Satyamurti, 'Enough That There Is'

Obsessions are compelling in art, especially when they lead to the kind of repetitiveness that increases our curiosity, rather than diminishes it. The poetic possibilities inherent in indulging obsessions – either with a particular subject-matter such as Gwyneth Lewis's birds, or theme, such as Carole Satyamurti's socio-political concerns – are well illustrated by these two authors' recent publications. In both, a strong sense of purpose and centrality prevails, the result of which is often a pleasing and admirable mix of subjectivity and objectivity.

Since winning the Aldeburgh Poetry Festival Prize in 1995, Gwyneth Lewis (Wales's first National Poet) has steadily gained recognition from critics as one of the most gifted writers of her generation. Two of her collections were short-listed for Forward prizes, and she has won several others including most recently the Cholmondeley Award in 2010. As well as a poet, Lewis is a librettist, which gives us a clue to her style. These poems work especially well if read aloud, when the lovely half-rhymes and alliteration are fully audible. On the page, the line-breaks can sometimes interrupt the phrasing, for example in this un-rhyming triplet from 'Quilting for Childless Women':

> Imagine a lake
> That doubles the view
> Of desolation –

Aloud, the line trips off the tongue joyfully. Yet Gwyneth Lewis's poems convey too much of a sense of their own making for these interruptions to be accidental. Indeed it is probably this sensitivity to her own craft which results in her tendency to shorten and separate out lines – and to break up the poems into separate sections. As the sequential pieces, 'Imaginary Walks in Istanbul', 'Quilting for Childless Women' and 'How to Knit a Poem' suggest, these short lines and stanzas represent real steps taken on an imaginative journey; as Anne Carson said of Sappho's fragments (one of which Lewis uses here as a title of her own poem), they imply "a free space of imaginal adventure."

The impression is of someone deeply involved in the process of making: "By now you know that I'm / A counter, and I do admire a square / With something in it," explains 'Imaginary Walks in Istanbul'. Here, Lewis is tellingly full of tenderness for the childhood ottoman: "A hard place, not designed for rest." Similarly, in 'How to Knit a Poem', commissioned by Radio 4, the poet advises: "The whole thing starts with a single knot / And needles. Word and Pen. Tie a loop / In nothing. Look at it. Cast on, repeat // The procedure till you have a line / That you can work with."

As this poem implies, Gwyneth Lewis is extremely adept at perceiving the potential in raw material, even if it's "nothing". Her scruples about respecting her sources do not however prevent her from making use of whatever she can, to create something new. This is exemplified in the 'quilt' poems, where titles from an exhibition of quilts at the de Young Museum, San Francisco, become starting points for a twelve-part sequence. It is especially evident in her bird series, where in 'What Do Birds Say?', for example, the speaker happily and symbolically strikes a balance between her own being and the bird's: "On Sunday I heard / The sparrow say, / 'We!'"

Carole Satyamurti has also been shortlisted for a Forward Prize, and her work too makes use of found things, though hers are perhaps more personal: found memories, found places and stories, found emotions. Her anger and frustration about contemporary politics, especially the fighting of wars, is particularly palpable, and makes *Countdown* a collection not only full of feeling, but also of great relevance. "The great protector strutting to the rescue / is besotted with incendiary harm," she writes in her opening poem 'The Igneous Age', "The puppet sucks his thumb."

Her book contains two epigraphs: one from Geoffrey Hill and one from Bertolt Brecht. No doubt these indicate how central to Satyamurti's writing her strongly held opinions and preoccupations with social problems are. Interestingly, she has included an excellent rhyming version of Brecht's '*Die Legende vom toten Soldaten*', and while many of her poems are written in a plain, clean style, when Satyamurti uses form she does so very well. This is particularly the case in the dramatic, highly wrought 'Memorial', which may become one of those anthologised pieces the author eventually gets bored of being admired for. It is admirable though, not least for the way it so effectively links style, form and content.

In contrast, several other of the poems in this new collection are quite conversational in style. With that can sometimes come a limitation, so that the initial and promising idea behind a poem is not able to reach its full potential. Elsewhere however, Satyamurti's humanitarianism, her experience in sociological research, and her poetic alertness combine to produce a range of beautiful lines and striking imagery:

> They wait. They wait by diminishing fires.
> The human hand's a puny instrument
> with no pick or spade to hearten it,
> and this is not the first time the mountains
> have breathed the stink of unburied dead,
> inclined the sheer indifference of their faces.

This is from 'Clothing Aid', Satyamurti's poem about the 2005 earthquake in Pakistan. Certainly, in both of these new publications from Bloodaxe Books there is a definite sense of conscientiousness, not only morally or politically but also linguistically. Both poets have a keen eye on the art – and artifice – of their craft; both are aware of the strange mix of "casting and purling" it involves.

Tara Bergin is currently studying at Newcastle University for a PhD on Ted Hughes's translations of János Pilinszky.

Joy And Mourning

MOLLY PEACOCK

Tim Liardet, *The Storm House*, Carcanet, £9.95, ISBN 9781847770677;
John F. Deane, *The Eye of the Hare*, Carcanet, £9.95, ISBN 9781847770929;
Carola Luther, *Arguing with Malarchy*, Carcanet, £9.95, ISBN 9781847770936

Combining an investigation into the mysterious circumstances of his brother's death with a headlong rush into mourning, Tim Liardet devises a pugilistic lyricism in *The Storm House*. This accomplished poet crosses a tone of bewildered longing, (think of Tennyson's "an infant crying in the night / with no language but a cry") with brutally riveting imagery, like the flayed flesh of Francis Bacon's portraits, and slams through a series of gripping lyrics toward the finale, the restless thirty-two-sonnet title sequence. Remembered incidents mix with "deleted scenes" to generate torrents of extreme feeling – the storm – that are framed by the structure of a family – the figurative house – left with its metaphorical roof torn off.

In 'Like Slant Rain', the poet unabashedly addresses his brother. His loneliness invites a reader into the struggle of figuring it all out: the facts of their lives together as children, growing up into quite separate existences, the younger becoming a poet (and keeper of their invented childhood private language which now has only one speaker), the older at the fringes of society, unable to grow except into sometimes appalling violence. In the end, the "slant rain" "goes on falling and tearing, falling and tearing," dissolving words into tears. In the unforgettable 'Deleted Scene (The Frog)', Liardet's horrifyingly graceful couplets describe a frog drying up to its death, trapped in a tin inside a hot shed. "The terror lived in the shed, we knew." That frog returns to haunt in the sonnet sequence's thirteenth section: "So many old revenges / were swung from your belt like scalped frogs, some still alive / hooked through". These sonnets batter at their edges – a poet crafting what his emotions thrash against – and call many aspects of masculinity into question, especially with the graphic beating of an "old woman [...] rising from the puddle of her blood." But they also allow Liardet to work out the "moral arithmetic" that "distilled the rhythm and logic" of the brother's life "into a single act." In the final couplet of Sonnet 18 he wrestles with the inverted logic of violence somehow justifying itself: "It was justice that was energy, justice that was fuel; / it was justice that put the whip in the ferule."

But the lost brother's "impotent fury" at last becomes poetry's saving potency.

Liardet builds from rhythmical and symbolic fragments, making a poem like 'Deleted Scene (The Jug)' a threshold onto his process. In an altercation between a father and son, a jar is smashed to bits but, through this splendid poet's imagination, reassembles. *What happened?* might be the central question of all poetry that relies on memory – and what drives the thrillingly tumultuous *Storm House* is that the poet will never find out.

In the title poem of his fourth collection, *Eye of the Hare*, distinguished Irish poet John F. Deane, bent on sharing what he views as a sacramental act of existence with the animal, refuses to shoot a rabbit. With this, Deane embarks on his mission to evoke experiences and environments that are being erased, adopting a simple syntactic credo: make poems of quiet but precise naming. Like the craft of dry stone walling that disdains cement in favor of fitting the rock surfaces precisely, he lifts the nouns – people, animals, plants, and vocations he wishes to save – and enters them into lines built by emphasizing the first part of speech that any child learns. 'Birds, Beasts and Buttercups' is Deane's *ars poetica*: "I felt / like one must have felt in the morning of the world, with the pact / to tend and care, to register / the long day stretching towards a late grey light. This is where / I would push the poem to go". His nominative mode replicates the vitality of the characters in 'Weeds and Wilderness': a young girl in a "thick, white-wool gansie," Sergeant Ted, who "kept a brass key / in his waistcoat," Missie, with her "caw-voice" and her daughter Mamie, "so bent in spine her knuckles / tapped on the stone floor as she walked."

The consistently elegiac tone makes a gloaming of the imagination. 'Ever this Night' features a child in bed in a hypnogogic state saying "All through the night / I was island". The vibrant 'Body Parts', in which butterflies "gorge themselves on the nectaries of flowers", is a loosely assembled five-sonnet sequence that echoes Dante by beginning 'In the Dark Wood', psychologically and spiritually repeating the half-light atmospheres. This sense of twilight reflects the lowering of the light on much of Irish country life, especially on Achill Island, where the poet was born. In the final sequence 'Achill: the Island', Deane employs the glorious mouth music of place names, as in 'Goban Choire: the Sound': "flat-faced gunard, whirlpool, eddy, / man-swallowing gorge of ocean, gob, and strait, / *sceadamáin*, gurges, sund." His poems can stumble when they simply relay the "what happened" of contemporary experience, but they come into fully observed being when the poet not only refuses to shoot the wild grace of natural life, but reveres it.

The alluring poems in 'Part One: Cusp' of Carola Luther's *Arguing with Malarchy* release an ecstasy of vocabulary. Luther becomes both musician and magician in 'Dreaming the Dead', with lines like "to manifest light in the ululant slip of a quick desert snake." She displays a Rilkean sense of the body that can merge with its environment in 'Vernal', and a free-spirited repetition in 'he did sing'. Both a natural metaphorist in 'News', where she calls a heart "an old animal clipped by a car", and an easy sensualist in 'Owl Ear', where a couple "lay our habit-arm / across the bed in sleep", she keeps the poems exuding freshness. In the enticing 'Turn' the lover, like "Friday / falling in love", experiences a "sole shaped [...] turn of the heart." Luther can be moving, dramatic, and slightly surreal. In 'The Colour of Lilac', the violet merging of sky and sea matches a heart-stopping moment of public humiliation; in 'Inquiry', a scene of catastrophe unfurls through a weave of questions and answers.

The clean gorgeousness of the opening sequence, and the beautifully aphoristic poems of the coda at the end of Part Two, 'Acres', are the book's treasures. But what Luther positions as its central peak, the sequence of twelve poems from which the volume takes its title, lacks this lively energy. The arduous dialectic of the "Old Man" in 'Arguing with Malarchy' fails to counter the intuitive moves Luther makes in her lyric poems, where even the saddest and most serious seem to ride off currents of air. In 'Waiting for Cure', the poet herself says, "no substance but movement, depth but no weight, / this swarm an illusion of sadness maybe, a confusion".

Molly Peacock is a North American poet and non-fiction writer whose latest book of poetry is *The Second Blush* and most recent book of non-fiction is *The Paper Garden: Mrs. Delany Begins Her Life's Work at 72.*

Interventions In The Face
Of Apocalypse

HARRIET TARLO

Tilla Brading and Frances Presley, *Stone Settings*,
Odyssey Books & Other Press, £4.95, ISBN 9781897654002;
Adrienne Rich, *Tonight No Poetry Will Serve: Poems 2007-2010*,
WW Norton and Co, $24.95, ISBN 9780393079678;
Ed Roberson, *To See the Earth Before the End of the World*, Wesleyan
University Press, £20.50, ISBN 9780819569509;
JL Williams, *Condition of Fire*, Shearsman Books, £8.95, ISBN 9781848611450

You would have thought that if anyone has earned the right to speak over the years, Adrienne Rich, the veteran American poet, surely has. Yet her title, *Tonight No Poetry Will Serve*, raises the controversial question of whether poetry is capable of intervening in a darkening world, before the lights go out. From my reading of them at least, each of the poets considered in this review have addressed this question. To respond to it – to employ Rich's image, evocative of the writing craft and the long-term condition of writing – they must attempt to "diagram the sentence". That is, each must sharpen his or her own individual and distinctive poetic philosophy, form and language accordingly.

Rich is best known for feminist, lesbian and anti-war campaigns, conducted in poetry and prose; as a result her poetry has perhaps at times too closely resembled prose (and vice versa) for some readers' and critics' tastes. This is a sparser and sparer writing than her mid-career work, a poetry in which significant images, Rich's greatest strength as a poet, shine out with intensity as in the opening of the title poem:

> Saw you walking barefoot
> taking a long look
> at the new moon's eyelid

For me, there is still the problem of sound in reading Rich. Her verse, although adeptly structured in terms of line-endings and punctuation contributing to the carving of an argument, pays little attention to rhythm.

It simply does not sing, and seldom has done. Perhaps it's true that "No one writes lyric on a battlefield", as she says in 'Quarto', yet that poem ends with a little lyric that sings more than most on a common subject in this book, the struggle to remain a singer (poet):

> I'll tell you about the mermaid
> Sheds swimmable tail   Gets legs for dancing
> Sings like the sea with a chokes throat
> Knives straight up her spine
> Lancing every step
> There is a price
> There is a price
> For every gift
> And all advice

In this collection, Rich does not "flinch" from the "glare" (her words); she does not abandon poetry of witness and intervention, but examines protest culture, the "disappeared", poverty and above all war (its "antique" and eternal presence signified by repeated images from the The Iliad). Here is a collection well worth reading for Rich's long thinking on matters that matter and her refusal to compromise, even more so perhaps "now the only where is here" – as she writes in her "Sickbed Shores", a poem which evokes powerfully how it feels to be a *"sick body in a sick country"*.

Jennifer L. Williams's *Condition of Fire* was written "on the isle of Salina, one of the volcanic Aeolian Islands off the coast of Sicily in the Tyrrhenian Sea, said to be the home of the god of winds". This gives an immediate sense of the territory conveyed by the poems; a harsh but beautiful seascape evoked through its elemental nature and its mythic, particularly Ovidian, connections. Here we find the sort of clear, clean concise writing we can look down into, as generations of literary dreamers have looked into the various seas of the Mediterranean.

What do we find in the depths? A combination of philosophical pieces, some great list poems and poems about mythic personae, some reminiscent of H.D's modernist project of almost a century ago. The use of contemporary language gives an immediacy to these pieces; each word is well-chosen though there is a little too liberal a sprinkling of punctuation (particularly at the ends of lines) for the poems to flow as they might. Here's 'Herse's Wedding Day', a poem revisiting Ovid's account of Aglauros's attempt to protect her sister Herse from the attentions of Mercury:

Aglauros can hardly breathe for the barbed wire.
Her sister's happy face swims before her eyes.

Minerva shudders as she clambers from the gutter;
Envy's half-eaten snakes writhe at her ankles.

Mercury tucks a hyacinth into his lapel
walking towards Herse's door past poor Aglauros,
now a statue of Aglauros.

Even Minerva (Athena to the Greek rather than Roman readers among you), trying to hatch her own new monarch with the help of the sisters, is sadly impotent here. There's no cheerful feminist revisionism in this version, just as at the end of 'Io' where we find the transformed girl "a stunning cow. / Her father holds her soft face in his hands, / torn by relief and wishing she'd never been born." As a collection however, these are not bleak poems. The devotion to metamorphosis, the principle of change, sustains an inspiring dream or deluded fantasy of endless renewal and immortality in a world where we feel the chill threat of apocalypse: "What if you could change into anything? / What if you could live, and live, and live?"

Tilla Brading's and Frances Presley's *Stone Settings* is part of a long term collaborative project which finding multiple forms in site specific work and walks, individual books (see Presley's Shearsman volume, *Lines of Sight*, 2009), performances and even the erection of a plaque to the neglected woman archaeologist, Hazel Eardley-Wilmot, at North Molton on Exmoor. Weighty matters such as human interventions in landscape and global warming are considered through the local and specific, the Neolithic stone settings, rows, longstones and circles of Exmoor. Each poem consists of words and images placed carefully on open form A4 pages which evoke the shapes and structures of these fragile, threatened and mysterious stones (some are known only in old records and can no longer be found). What might they teach us about landscape and about ourselves? This poetry begins to and refuses to answer this question, ultimately making you want to put on your walking boots and go out to your own local stones to explore their mysteries.

The whole process has been described by Anna Reckin as "psycho-archaeology" (a term drawn from psycho-geography), which says much about the depth of engagement here. Brading and Presley work on site, but they also draw on numerous written sources. Human ways of engaging with places of the past (including the mythic, aetiological, historical, archeological and geometrical) appear fragmentarily, suggesting that all are in one way or another fallible. Source texts are treated with a wary respect and sympathy. In the preface to Dina Portway Dobson's *Archeology of Somerset*:

> Today the archeologist needs   attributes of the bird
>   or the mole
>
>   the help of an aeroplane
>
>   or a spade

Here the natural and unnatural are set against each other, in a witty spatialising of found prose text. Throughout this collection the range of language is diverse, playful and beautiful although, like much of this sort of work, hard to excerpt as words and phrases overlap and echo throughout the collection. 'Brer' evokes the sense of sonic patterning:

> bre-er
> out of the briar patch
> sweet briar
> out of the bare earth
> he came
> brer
>
> an edge
> e
> merge
> an angle

In recent committed poetry, particularly ecopoetics, I've noticed a move towards the collaborative text and the use of found text; a shift away from the idea that individual voices might be enough to find a way though our predicament. This is about looking back as well forward, finding voices worth hearing or worth interrogating from the past. It's a risky business, especially when you add the variables of weather and place to it, as Brading and Presley do ("anticipation and disappointment / part of the project"), but it produces original poetry with a porous sense of person, language and place.

Global environmental crisis is at the heart of Ed Roberson's poetry. He has observed it in places as diverse as Alaska, Afognak Island, Bermuda, the Andes, Mexico, the Caribbean, Nigeria and West Africa. Yet all this travel has an air of desperation about it: "People are grabbing the chance to see / the earth before the end of the world, / the world's death piece by piece each longer than we". *To See the Earth Before the End of the World* is really five books in one, and hence a useful British introduction to Roberson's fine work. Three of the five deal with the earth in large philosophical terms. I miss, a little, the sense of place, of local landscape detail that we find in Presley/Brading, but Roberson is adept at starting simply and then luring you into deeper levels of thought about the world. "The red spot on two mating cranes" is a fine example; what seem to be real birds shift into the realisation that this is "someone dressed up like nature / trying to dance up a future". The poem and this contemporary tribal ritual constructed to attempt to save a bird. It is these shifting perspectives, horizons and, above all, the sense of lost balance which is at the heart of these poems. Roberson's big summative lines are well-earned: "We look upon the world to see ourselves", "water is the skin of the earth". The two other parts, a fascinating set of poems playing on film, photography and racial politics and a section featuring some fine poems on music and urban life, are also well worth reading. Roberson is a shape-shifter of a poet – it's a pleasure to watch his finding the form for the poem as he works, using space and stanza form with subtlety and grace.

Harriet Tarlo recently edited *The Ground Aslant: An Anthology of Radical Landscape Poetry* (Shearsman, 2011); her fourth poetry collection is due from Shearsman in 2012.

Lift Off

SARAH WARDLE

Claire Potter, *Swallow*, Five Islands Press, £7.20, ISBN 9780734041593;
Rachael Boast, *Sidereal*, Picador, £8.99, ISBN 9780330513395;
Kit Fan, *Paper Scissors Stone*, Hong Kong University Press,
£8.95, ISBN 9789888083473

Claire Potter's mesmerising debut collection, *Swallow*, is a fine first book, whose lines dart and dip like the migrating and home-building bird. Her presentation is experimental, yet the pace achieved by the pauses, indentations and line-spaces is one of a natural, unforced, speech rhythm. To read this book is to be calmed and charmed by its poet.

The poems bear a second and third reading, which elicit further meanings. Potter has an ear for the musical phrase: "Love's hands up in throes: / ants write in moving water what between us / cannot be disclosed". She also has an ear for the unfolding clauses of syntax, even where she disrupts expectation. She voices love and disappointment, alongside memory and thought: "It is not / that you will not return (today, yesterday, tomorrow [...])." *Swallow* is filled with her native Australia's landscapes and nature, as well as inspired by Europe and America. Its lines are rich in allusion and inter-textuality, imagery and alliteration, and seem "born / out of the etcetera of human relations, not / asked either way". Though Potter does not explore the other senses and associations of the word "swallow", her language at times sings and rises like the bird.

Rachael Boast's finely-phrased first collection, *Sidereal*, announces a rising star of British poetry. Her lyricism has dark depths: "for it's not love that's evasive, / it's the years spent void of course, / perfecting a face in the empty mirrors/ of memory". In 'Syzygy' she gets up to "walk the streets at four in the morning", when "The night sky sometimes likes a good conversation, / and gives me plenty of time to speak before thinking". Blake's illustrations, the landscape of Iceland and the suffering of Job are some of her themes. Ideas of determinism and divine retribution lead the poet to haunting statements, such as "some clean change claimed me", and memorable questions, such as "Who to believe when Yahweh doesn't appear?" and "why does the heart furl / like a winter rose, withdraw / when it means to disclose?"

In 'Falls of Inversnaid' Boast writes that the water "believes, cannot do other / than turn towards its larger cause". Elsewhere, she says, "I'd live the night out / on the dark hymnal lake, to hear it talking / towards the edges of itself – that voice of the waters". It is as if water had a transparent mind that broods within it and represents conscience, or consciousness. *Sidereal* is at once a spiritual and earthly book, deftly crafted and celestially inspired.

Kit Fan's assured first collection is *Paper Scissors Stone*, for which he won the inaugural Hong Kong University Poetry Prize. His book moves from a creation-of-language myth to a translation of Chinese poetry, yet he looks far beyond his native Hong Kong and China to the British Library, Dublin, classical culture, politics, upheaval and war – and their effects. In 'Thatched House Destroyed by an Autumn Storm' he translates Tu Fu, an eighth-century poet, who wondered, "how many houses we'd need to build / to shelter the world's poor". In 'BN(O)', that is British National (Overseas), he observes "the silence of refugees longing for an identity".

Fan's poems are at the same time meditative and relevant. He writes of the light of the world and its shadows, of breeze and storm, with wit and sorrow. Traditions overlap and energize each other. In *Paper Scissors Stone* languages, nations, peoples and cultures meet, as at a crossroads. The title poem concerns the transitory nature of reading and writing itself, as the poet's childhood library is torn down and he contemplates "why paper / attracts scissors, books turn to stone". Kit Fan skilfully draws together people, places and times through an articulate, complex and poised poetry.

Sarah Wardle's *A Knowable World* appeared in 2009.

Double Lives

ANGEL DAHOUK

Roberto Bolaño, trans. Laura Healy, *The Romantic Dogs*,
Picador, £8.99, ISBN 9780330510677;
Garrison Keillor, *77 Love Sonnets*, Bloodaxe, £12, ISBN 9781852249007;
Alfred Brendel, trans. Alfred Brendel and Richard Stokes, *Collected Poems of Alfred Brendel: Playing the Human Game*, Phaidon,
£24.95, ISBN 9780714859866

In spite of its elitist reputation, poetry is an art form that many people turn their hand to, including actors, politicians, and media personalities. Chilean-born Roberto Bolaño, who died in 2003, is best known as a novelist. He has become an icon for students, a staple of public transport readers. What is less well-known is that he was first and foremost a poet, who had been forced to accept fiction's wider currency in order to provide for his family. *The Romantic Dogs*, a selection of Bolaño's poetry between 1980 and 1998, captures the essence of Bolaño's narratives, as the reader is confronted with cursory portraits of unwashed characters, and rapid accounts of dreams and desperation. This bilingual archive is the study without which the novels could not exist. The poems are at once simplistic and diligent. They trek from youthful fervour and revolution across reality and wretchedness, ultimately alighting on the hope that can only grow out of poverty and loss. "Poets of Troy", exclaims Bolaño in his final poem, "Nothing that could have been yours / Exists anymore... / You are free".

Bolaño's free verse roams from past to present, from one city to the next, taking in the tragedy of lost Chile and replaying scenes from 1970s Mexico City. Along the way, we encounter vernacular characters – Lupe the teenage hooker, the worm with "an assassin's glare", and the anti-poet Nicanor Parra all lost in "the motionless mud [...] / in the rose of nothingness". Using little variation, Laura Healy produces a literal translation of Bolaño's text, which might suggest mere idle decoding, but here she honours the raw eloquence in Bolaño's stark choice of words. "Underdevelopment", suggests Bolaño in *Bomb magazine* (2001), "only allows for great works of literature".

Ironically, the romance in Bolaño's reimagining of the world is far more moving than the narcissism apparent in Garrison Keillor's loose sonnet forms. Bolaño's poetry draws out invisible lives, and the richness of culture, while Keillor's verse is repetitive and parochial. On the reverse title of *77 Love Sonnets*, Keillor begs his readers' pardon should they take offence. These sonnets, however, are too banal to offend; sculpted with unblinking bourgeois conceit. While Bolaño looks outward, Keillor's vision is picket-fenced. Keillor has made a name for himself on the radio but also as an anthologist. His love of sonnets sprung from an assignment that required him to commit Shakespeare's Sonnet No. 29 to memory at the age of sixteen. That age seems significant since both the content and construction of his sonnets emit the earnestness of adolescence. In one poem he describes a childhood flame, Christine, by remembering how she stood in front of him in choir: "I smelled her exotic French cologne / And felt the existential heat of her body, / I became Luciano Pavarotti". Attempting to reinvent an archaic art form, Keillor chooses a combination of personal recollection and current affairs, introducing both humour and topical figureheads. By way of example, Obama is granted a full fourteen lines: "We cried, old black ladies and me, and applauded, / We wept, America, for you justified / At last as a nation of by God true ideals".

Ranging from patriotism to desire, Keillor endeavours to capture differing types of love through tired themes, such as food, to which he adds nothing fresh or uncontrived. In 'Supper', Keillor dines with a lover by candlelight on "salmon with dill / And lemon and whole-wheat couscous / Baked with garlic and fresh ginger, and a hill / Of green beans and carrots roasted with honey and tofu". Eroticism takes hold in 'The Beach', where Keillor shamelessly likens the female to "a pink anemone" which tastes of "caviar and Cabernet". Yet underlying his notions of romance remain the hardline beliefs which he previously made explicit in *The Baltimore Sun* (2009) when he announced, "Christmas is a Christian holiday – if you're not in the club, then buzz off". Keillor's sonnets read like a foot being squeezed into a shoe two sizes too small. Lacking both substance and rhythm, he ultimately renders the sonnet a redundant form.

Unlike Bolaño and Keillor, Alfred Brendel is not unused to seeing his poems in print, although his name is better known among musicians. He has published a number of poetry volumes, which are collected in *Playing the Human Game* alongside the original German. Brendel himself undertakes the role of translator, collaborating once again with the celebrated linguist Richard Stokes. Born in Czechoslovakia in 1931, and a resident of the UK since 1970, Brendel is one of the world's most eminent pianists. On paper, he composes surreal verses which, in his *Collected*, are sectioned into fifteen pairings, some more common (Angels and Devils), some more curious (Buddhas and Santas). "I am not exclusively a musician", says Brendel, "I now lead a kind of double life", and he reiterates this in 'Hybrid' where he admits, "that's what you're dealing with / a Jekyll and Hyde".

It is a blessing that Brendel has turned to poetry; his imagination is a complex yet playful hangout. Brendel explains a difficult world by drawing out the humour in the absurd, in a way that sometimes borders on the slapstick, Brendel explains a difficult world by drawing out the humour in the absurd. "And once again / the Lord of the universe / recorded a day of good works / three religious wars launched / several tornados unleashed / a new brand of pestilence devised [...] / countless children successfully harmed". While each poem is named in the Contents, the pages themselves do not carry titles. Each section carries a sequence of uninterrupted free verse with punctuation making a rare appearance, reinforcing the idea that events and encounters cannot conform to familiar frameworks. The overt humour is offset by subtle moments that reveal a solid pessimism beneath the laughter. This becomes particularly apparent in a series of love poems, which Brendel introduces by announcing abruptly, "The moment has arrived / to write a love poem". His imagery here is both distinctive and gloriously unexpected: "Suddenly it has become simple / to lose yourself in love / One day / you look for yourself / and find nothing [...] / heart over heels / a doting astronaut". Crossing from love to death, his imagery becomes ever more charged and poignant: birdsong in 'The Gallows-bird' is described as "fervent like a circular saw / whose motor suddenly cuts out".

Its poems interspersed with paintings and photographs, including one of a stuffed baby crocodile donning a bonnet and bow, *Playing the Human Game* is a brilliantly surreal and penetrating collection. Brendel's pianist's fingers are effortlessly poetic, revealing him to be a master of the double life.

Angel Dahouk holds an MA in Cultural Policy and was recently a visiting lecturer on poetry education at City University.

AMONG OUR CONTRIBUTORS

Emily Berry won an Eric Gregory Award in 2008. Her pamphlet is *Stingray Fevers* (Tall-Lighthouse). **Malika Booker** is the first Poet in Residence at the Royal Shakespeare Company. **Alan Brownjohn**'s *The Saner Places: Selected Poems* (Enitharmon) has just appeared. **John Burnside**'s *Black Cat Bone* (Cape) is shortlisted for the Forward Prize. **Olivia Byard**'s *Strange Horses* (Flambard) appears in October. **Kevin Crossley-Holland**'s *The Mountains of Norfolk: New and Selected Poems* (Enitharmon) appears this autumn. **James Byrne**'s second collection is *Blood/Sugar* (Arc 2009). He edits *The Wolf* and was recently a Stein Fellow at New York University. **Eugene Dubnov** was born in Estonia. *Thousand Year Minutes* (Shoestring), with Anne Stevenson, appears next year. **Antony Dunn**'s third collection is *Flying Fish and Bugs* (Carcanet). **Kit Fan** won the inaugural International HKU Poetry Prize and his first book of poems *Paper Scissors Stone* was published by Hong Kong University Press (March). **Isabel Galleymore** graduated from St Andrews with an MLitt in Poetry in 2011. **Alyson Hallett**'s latest collection is *The Stone Library* (Peterloo). **W.N. Herbert**, with Yang Lian, is editing *Jade Ladder*, an anthology of contemporary Chinese poetry (Bloodaxe, 2012). He is Professor of Poetry and Creative Writing at Newcastle University. **Fanny Howe**'s most recent publications include *Come and See* and *The Winter Sun*, both from Graywolf. **Maria Jastrzębska**'s most recent collection is *Everyday Angels* from Waterloo Press. *Dementia Diaries* is on tour with Lewes Live Literature. **Terry Jones**'s first collection, *Furious Resonance*, was published by Poetry Salzburg in June. **Gwyneth Lewis**'s most recent book is *Sparrow Tree* (Bloodaxe Books, 2011), she is currently a Visiting Fellow at Girton College, Cambridge. **Maitreyabandhu** has won the Keats-Shelley, Basil Bunting, Geoffrey Dearmer and Ledbury Festival prizes. **Glyn Maxwell**'s *One Thousand Nights and Counting: Selected Poems* (Picador) appeared this spring. **John Mole** is Poet in the City's current poet-in-residence. His most recent collection is *The Point of Loss* (Enitharmon, 2011). **Robert Saxton** is the author of three poetry collections and a version of the Greek poet Hesiod in 80 sonnets, entitled *Hesiod's Calendar* (Carcanet). **Seni Seneviratne**'s *The Heart of It* will be available in March 2012 from Peepal Tree Press. **Anne Stevenson** won the Lannan Lifetime Achievement Award in 2007. *Astonishment* is forthcoming in 2012. **ko ko thett** is 'a poet by choice and Burmese by chance'. He is also an activist and analyst and has lectured, written, and commented extensively on Burma since the late 1990s. **Lizzi Thistlethwayte**'s pamphlet is *No Map* (2009). **Siriol Troup**'s *Beneath the Rime*, was published by Shearsman in 2009. **Ahren Warner**'s first collection, *Confer* (Bloodaxe) is both a Poetry Book Society Recommendation and shortlisted for the Forward Prize for Best First Collection. **Yang Lian** is Professor at the European Graduate School in Saas-Fee, Switzerland; his ten collections have been translated into more than twenty languages.

THE POETRY SOCIETY

NATIONAL
★ POETRY ★
COMPETITION

N.P.C.

LOVE

1ST
★ Prize ★
£5000

JUDGES: COLETTE BRYCE, JOHN GLENDAY & JACKIE KAY
ENTER AT: WWW.POETRYSOCIETY.ORG.UK   DEADLINE: 31 OCTOBER 2011

ROLL UP! ROLL UP! THE DEADLINE IS FAST APPROACHING...